DATE			

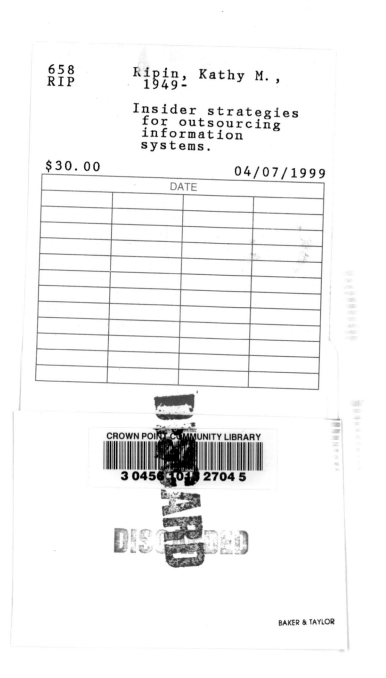

Insider Strategies for
Outsourcing Information Systems

Insider Strategies
for Outsourcing
Information Systems

Building Productive Partnerships,
Avoiding Seductive Traps

Kathy M. Ripin
Leonard R. Sayles

Oxford   New York
Oxford University Press
1999

Oxford University Press

Oxford   New York
Athens   Auckland   Bangkok   Bogotá   Buenos Aires   Calcutta
Cape Town   Chennai   Dar es Salaam   Delhi   Florence   Hong Kong   Istanbul
Karachi   Kuala Lumpur   Madrid   Melbourne   Mexico City   Mumbaí
Nairobi   Paris   São Paulo   Singapore   Taipei   Tokyo   Toronto   Warsaw

and associated companies in
Berlin   Ibadan

Copyright © 1999 by Oxford University Press, Inc.

Published by Oxford University Press, Inc.
198 Madison Avenue, New York, NY 10016

Oxford is a registered trademark of Oxford University Press

Library of Congress Cataloging-in-Publication Data is Available
ISBN 0-19-512566-5

1 3 5 7 9 8 6 4 2
Printed in the United States of America
on acid-free paper.

For William R. Yeack
Who inspired, supported, and enriched
our work with his vast experience and wisdom

Contents

Preface

Every company and its managers are under unremitting pressures to improve performance. Insatiable corporate expectations reflect an unforgiving stock market and a brutal global economy. One result is the increasing emphasis being placed on ever more sophisticated and well-targeted information systems. Timely, accurate, "user-friendly" information has become the managerial engine powering continuous change to facilitate world-class operations, innovative marketing, and customer service. These increasingly powerful computer-based decision tools are being designed and supported by experienced "outsourcers," also known as contractors/vendors.

This book describes how user/managers can work with outside technology experts to capitalize on the incredible power, flexibility, and adaptability of new computer-based information systems. Paradoxically, these demanding systems can also free managers to take risks, be innovative, and experiment—when designed and implemented with a focus on users.

Fair warning: we begin with some harsh reality—the results of outsourcer designed and supported critical system investments are often disappointing. In this fast-changing, technology-driven business environment, most managers optimistically assume they can shuck off most of the frustrations and complexities of information systems by using outsourcers. They delight in the belief: "Now it's their problem." Their widely experienced specialists will take responsibility for the intimidating, costly, and endless vexations associated with information systems management. But in a surprisingly large number of cases, outsourced system costs are greater and performance is less than anticipated, enhancement is difficult, and even total failure is not rare. Getting changes (not covered by the contract) implemented can require tough negotiations.

Managers at all levels have a big stake in how effectively their companies cope with the outsourcing of information systems (IS). The ease and competence with which executives can do their jobs and the quality of their decisions increasingly are dependent on the work of IS vendors. This is a book that tells managers how to collaborate effectively with outsourcers to obtain and maintain systems that work to their everyday advantage, not their constant frustration. Managers will learn how well-targeted involvement and control in outsourcing enables them to play a critical role in fine-tuning and enhancing these systems. And senior executives will find experience-based guidelines enabling them to realistically assess outsourcer sales claims while avoiding the seductive myths and illusions that distort contractor selection and new system planning decisions. We detail the most frequent sources of new system failure and include compelling detailed case examples of how astute users and their outsourcers can avoid these traps and produce superb results.

The cases we present will aid vendors, the contractors and outsourcers, in becoming more realistic about building client partnerships: how to work collaboratively with users and increase both the sophistication and realism of their clients. Our emphasis is on integrating the complementary skills and knowledge of the inside user with the outside expert. As our cases demonstrate, good outsourcing results in systems that are "works in progress," encouraging client-initiated fine-tuning, enhancement, and change.

We identify the tough implementation problems and the strategic issues in outsourcing information systems. We make explicit the behavioral skills and solutions that have proven effective in a wide variety of business settings. We also include a rare insider view of the tortured dynamics of typical systems development projects. Our examples run the gamut from new application software and outsourced operations to enterprise-wide systems. Throughout, we use everyday English and avoid arcane terminology.

Where the Data and Conclusions Come From

We undertook a multi-year study of a number of large U.S. and overseas systems integration projects. In the course of this work, we interviewed a number of experienced outsourcer project managers. These superbly skilled professionals provided candid accounts of what went wrong—or right—on the major projects on which they had worked. In addition to this fieldwork, we drew on our own project management and consulting experience that has emphasized the challenge of introducing new technologies. With one exception, we have not been able to obtain permission to use actual company names in the examples we cite. The industry, technology, and sequence of events, however, represent accurate accounts of what occurred in the dozens of cases we use to develop our conclusions.

Authors and Contributors

Ripin has been a line manager/user and sponsor of outsourcing contracts in a major financial services company; she has a Master's from Columbia University's Graduate School of Business, and now heads a consulting firm that specializes in the interaction of new information systems technology and customer service. Sayles, Professor Emeritus of Management, Graduate School of Business, Columbia University, has an MIT doctorate and substantial experience studying the problems of implementing new technologies. His many field-research-based books have become standard references for executives and MBA students around the world and have received major awards from management professional societies and corporate groups.

We both have been fortunate in having Bill Yeack as a guide to this fast-changing, complex field. His extraordinary knowledge base and generous encouragement have been indispensable. Yeack has been responsible for the management of more than fifty major software development projects in Europe and Asia as well as America. He has occupied senior managerial positions with Tandem Computers and Andersen Consulting and had both the vision and the courage to give outsiders access to the most challenging systems development projects. He recognized that these demanding multimillion-dollar projects had complexities that stretched the usefulness of standard project management techniques. Their managers had to meet extraordinarily demanding specifications while contending with intricate interrelationships among contractors, subcontractors, clients, and their users.

We were also the beneficiaries of extraordinary assistance from a number of broadly experienced professionals who have successfully managed the challenging design and implementation of innovative information systems. Our appreciation is small compensation for their many hours of discussion with us. Al Fisher, Don Poirier, and Jean Baptiste Dupont combine a high level of managerial skill with the ability (and patience) to reconstruct their complex projects, some extending over many years. They contributed some of our most important case material. Mark Aukman was also most helpful in recounting his experiences with a major outsourcer. Cynthia Smith and Sam Brown lent their technical and managerial knowledge in reviewing early drafts of this manuscript. Brown has evaluated systems investments for a major financial services company. Trained as an anthropologist, Dr. Smith became an indispensable collaborator in some of our fieldwork and generously shared her cross-cultural project experiences.

It would be nice to say that, in retrospect, the four years involved in completing this work were continuously satisfying. That would not be true as many long-suffering friends could testify. Fortunately, Herb Addison, our Oxford editor, made the final stage a most pleasant one.

Dobbs Ferry, New York
December 1998

Insider Strategies for
Outsourcing Information Systems

The What, Why, and How of
Outsourcing Information Systems

As they experience ever more intense competition, almost all companies have the same strategic priority: becoming more focused on service, quality, and operational excellence. In today's computer-based business world, accomplishment will depend, in part, on an organization's ability to become more effective in its use of information systems (IS). Paradoxically, the growing dependence on information systems is accompanied by ever-greater use of outsourcers both to design and to manage this critical resource. This seems like a profound inconsistency.

Over the years, truly successful companies have been those with management able to confront and cope with anomalies and contradictions. That may, in fact, be the best test of managerial excellence. It separates those who simply "go with the flow" — usually not even recognizing the contradictions inherent in their strategies — from executives who can develop creative solutions to tough dilemmas.

Executives, alert to these dilemmas, will have found ways to make outsourced information systems responsive to their rapidly changing requirements. They recognize that an essential component of an operational excellence strategy is the development of the line manager's capacity and motivation to use systems to continuously enhance performance.

In less successful companies, outsourced systems have become an administrative encumbrance. Their managers increasingly ignore the need for fine-tuning and walk away from information technology issues. Their systems are the outsourcers' "business." These managerial challenges are the subject of this book. ⏎ENTER

Outsourcing as the Obvious Answer

Executives, particularly senior managers, are almost unanimous in recognizing the numerous advantages to outsourcing components of their companies' information systems and computer technology. Long-standing frustrations with these technologies, their accelerating costs and intimidating future requirements, the scarcity of the unique expertise required—all favor letting experienced outsiders bear the brunt of managing this "bear."

Managers increasingly appear to have a love/hate relationship with their computer systems. The powerful and flexible information systems they make possible have become indispensable. Few actions are taken in modern business without a computer-based contribution. Not surprisingly, organizations are devoting increasing percentages of their annual budgets to new hardware and software.

There is a simultaneous dark side to this nonstop growth in the importance of information systems: management's unease with their dependency on these volatile technologies as well as a sense of vulnerability. Accompanying the extraordinary costs are the threats of investments that don't pay off, occasional devastating failure, and rapid obsolescence.

Probably a majority of American companies have outsourced or are planning to outsource everything from the maintenance of their mainframes and desktops to the design and development of new enterprise-wide information systems that will integrate diverse business functions or structure "data warehouses."[1] External service providers (outsources) have become the critical resource for developing new, more powerful systems, enhancing (or "fixing") existing systems and operating some or all of the components of a company's information system. Even technology-savvy companies like Lucent have outsourced a great deal of their information technology (IT) management.

Not surprisingly, systems development has become one of the fastest growing industries in America. Multibillion-dollar outsourcing contracts are no longer unusual. Almost 10% of expenditures for information technology probably involve an outsourcer. With increasing frequency, the business press announces yet another company seeking contracts in this field. The large players include such familiar names as IBM Global Services, EDS, Andersen Consulting, AT&T Solutions, Computer Sciences, and the Europeans like SAP and Cap Gemini.

Strong Inducements

Although some CEOs are beginning to get their "feet wet," learning to feel comfortable with PCs—even using them—many of their organizations are still running scared. Their costly, sophisticated new technologies appear to be controlling them, not the reverse. The decision to outsource seems simple and obvious. Outsourcers are promising big savings in annual IT and IS costs. And some companies even believe that the only real control they need is in overseeing annual contract costs.

Outsourcing information systems is also part of the extraordinary course reversal in American business's strategic thinking. Not many years ago, companies wanted to own everything that contributed to their operations. Today, shedding all so-called non-core functions is one of the highly publicized hallmarks of astute management.

Information Systems Move from Back Office to Front Office. The critical reasons for outsourcing have a great deal to do with the evolution of user-friendlier, user-relevant technologies. Mainframe-based systems, "back office" computers, have traditionally provided transaction processing and record keeping. Managers now demand everyday usability: flexible, adaptable information systems that will allow them to have easy (random) access to data, customized analytical tools, and integration of information residing in diverse data banks. Many of these systems should enable the company to integrate and more tightly coordinate diverse business functions and diverse geographic locations. And all of this should be presented in easy-to-use and readily changeable formats. Managers also need systems that readily incorporate new products and markets and adapt to acquisitions and divestments.

Guilt by Association. Many companies that outsource believe that their internal IS and IT staffs do not have the knowledge to successfully implement fast-changing client/server technology and the extraordinarily demanding enterprise-wide systems. And they associate their existing staff with all the rigidities of their legacy systems. (A classic complaint: "It would take us literally months to get what seemed like a trivial software change when we introduced a product modification. And forget it if you complain that a format isn't user friendly.")

Companies are reluctant to hire new systems analysts and programmers. At the same time, the ranks of insider software specialists are being depleted as these "overhead" departments fall victim to corporatewide downsizing. Programs to retrain and update existing staffs are in short supply. This reluctance also predisposes companies to turn to external service providers when their information systems need upgrading.

The Neglected Side of Outsourcing

But few issues, particularly managerial ones, are simple. There is a profoundly important other side to outsourcing computer technology. Management can't outsource its responsibility for these systems, its need to understand these new technologies and take ownership. As tempting as it may be to feel that the outsider will do it all, management cannot walk away. Client managers have critically demanding roles to play if the outsourcing is going to meet company expectations and objectives.

Why Information Systems Are Part of Any Company's "Core"

Information systems are part of the very core of any business, and critical inputs from business managers are required both in their design and operation. After all, these systems deal with information and communications. In the information age, these "crown jewels" are indispensable inputs for managerial decision making as well as the underpinning of many mission-critical company operations. As many have noted, successful companies, particularly those in service industries, increasingly are information technology driven.

The foundation of corporate reengineering is integrating what had been discrete business functions. For example, the input of new orders may automatically trigger changes in factory floor scheduling and parts inventory. This coordination is dependent on a smoothly functioning information system.

The strategic initiatives of the most innovative organizations in dynamic industries draw some of their strength from their carefully crafted information systems. Reacting to highly competitive markets, astute executives push for ever-faster adaptation, innovation, and cost reduction while stressing more attention to customer satisfaction. Information technology is at the heart of company efforts to promote these goals. Thus, in a relatively short period of time, companies have had to absorb two profound changes in how they do business: the impact of computer technology and the outsourcing of major components of this new driving force.[2]

Accelerating Costs

The combined effect of downsizing and reengineering has been that many companies now find that their labor costs are relatively stable, even declining, but their information technology costs are increasing annually at an intimidating rate. Banking is an excellent example of the importance of technology and technology costs. In 1996, the Tower Group estimated that Citicorp spent close to 2 billion on technology with Chase not far behind at 1.8 billion in that one year![3]

Substantial managerial leadership and knowledge about the key issues in outsourcing of information technology are essential for ensuring that outsourced information systems stay consistent with business strategies. Even when the initial requirements are well conceived, products, markets, and services change, and companies acquire and divest. At the same time, the panoply of information technology available keeps evolving and investment soars. The costs and potential contributions of information technology have become so consequential that senior executives, willingly or unwillingly, now devote major executive energies to IS and IT strategies. *And, as later chapters describe, outsourcing doesn't change that requirement.*

A Problem Coming Out of the Closet

Most of what has been written about outsourcing focuses on purely technical software and hardware issues or on somewhat simplistic cost/benefit calculations and the intricacies of contract writing. Very little attention has been paid to the managerial decisions that are required to make outsourcing work effectively to further business goals (in contrast to financial or information technology objectives).

A Ground Swell of Dissatisfaction.   There is mounting evidence of client dissatisfactions and costly failures in the outsourcing of the development of new systems and their operations. The rush to outsource these vexing technologies and eliminate the concomitant managerial frustrations can dull sensitivity to all the warning signals that outsourcing is less easy than it may appear. To be fair, many of what we call warning signals have been well hidden. While consulting firms like the Gartner Group have publicized the failure of many companies to exercise due diligence and then experience disappointments, little mention is made of disgruntled customers and performance problems in the mainstream management publications (in contrast to magazines for IS and IT specialists).[4]

Outsourcing can be a very useful strategy, but it can also be a high-risk endeavor. In our research we found few companies prepared to cope with the major challenges or even aware of the complexities they were about to confront. Perhaps the relief they experienced knowing that the real experts would be taking over these intimidating, volatile technologies blinded them. And senior executives usually felt uneasy, even intimidated, about the impenetrable (and "unseeable") software underlying information systems.

A Survival Guide for Managers Involved in Outsourcing

The research that backs up our work and our writing focuses on the subtle and often misunderstood managerial skills now demanded in the five groups of key participants who make or break an outsourced information system initiative:

1. Client managers who must make major outsourcing decisions. These are the choices of what is to be done by whom and their time and financial parameters—and how the whole process will be monitored and evaluated.

2. Client IS and IT professionals who provide specialized counsel and critical inputs to design and operations and are often the technical linkages between the client and outsourcer organizations.

3. The line managers who are the actual users of these information systems and depend on them to meet their performance goals.

4. Outsourcer professionals: systems designers and analysts, programmers, and project architects.

5. Outsourcer project and program managers.

Most of these participants will find themselves troubled and challenged by many of the dilemmas and paradoxes inherent in the outsourcing of information technology—in contrast to the outsourcing of assembly components or payroll services. Managing and measuring software and systems development (e.g., how close to perfection? how easy to improve? how vulnerable? how much should it cost?) are inherently frustrating and answers are elusive. It is not surprising to see managers and professionals struggling to come to terms with issues like the following.

- Managing information technologies can be a serious distraction for line executives; after all, these systems are only facilitators, support functions. Increasingly, however, the intimate details of the design and operation of these systems profoundly impact the effectiveness of most business operations. And the details of the business need to inform the design and operation of the system. Only user/managers fully comprehend current business requirements and their strategic importance.

- The trend toward outsourcing these technologies shows every sign of increasing. But information and communications are the very lifeblood of every company, the underpinning of any sensible managerial decision. How can "outsiders" handle this strategic resource best?

- Managers understandably seek to be decisive and it is very satisfying to "settle" these frustrating technology questions by saddling them on a responsible outsider. But both business needs and technology itself are highly dynamic; today's decision can be obsolete next month.

- Management wants outside experts—their outsourcer—to build (and often operate) these new systems. But increasing evidence indicates that the most effective relationships between outsourcer and client are those in which the users' understanding of and ability to influence directly their own systems' enhancements are strengthened. Such skill building and strategic change have to grow out of an appreciation of the mutual interdependence of client and vendor.

- Most management "principles" presume some clearly definable product, service, or contribution. New information systems are only as good as users can make them (by their ingenuity in application). And many, if not most, information systems depend on creativity; they are "works in progress," never finished. Thus, there is no easy way to compartmentalize the work of the outsourcer from the work of the client and user.

Required: A New Kind of Partnering

The essence of outsourcing something as critical as the company's information processing and communication involves the development of a partnership. But the requirement is a unique kind of relationship that most executives are not prepared to execute. It is far removed from appealingly definitive "go"/"no go" decisions. This may reflect the reality that partnering has become a management mantra and therefore has lost meaning. In this globally competitive postindustrial world almost every company proudly proclaims its new "partner(s)." But partnering in the development and operation of information systems is profoundly more difficult than working with a contractor who is going to provide a subassembly for a new tennis shoe. These are extraordinarily demanding technologies: dynamic, often quite volatile, delicate—subject to lots of unanticipated glitches and well-hidden vulnerabilities. Many information systems force business to adapt to the new technology, not the reverse.

No one doubts that computers are a permanent mainstay of business, although their software and hardware will change dramatically. Given their centrality and ever-increasing costs, every management has to learn how to get inside outsourcing.

Unquestionably, outsourcers provide enormous assistance in developing new computer-based management and decision support systems and operating and maintaining them. In performing these functions, they can (and should) be educating line managers on what these emerging technologies can do—and how they do it. Users have to be "in the loop." But these vendors can't teach managers what their businesses should be doing, what the technology should be accomplishing. No matter who facilitates systems design and/or operations, it is still the inside management, not the outside contractor, who needs to be making choices—at conception and forever after.

Our First Conclusions

- Senior management fools itself when it categorizes the design and management of company information systems as not being "core" functions of the business.

- Reengineering, the emphasis on process and flow, in contrast to traditional functions, is how most companies are now organizing themselves and they often have information systems as their foundation.

- The most significant variable costs in many corporations are now their information processing, computer and systems design, and maintenance costs, *not* labor costs.

- The intimidating complexities of information systems technologies have created a rush to outsource.

- Few companies seem to be aware of the complexities of outsourcing itself. And there is little recognition of the high rate of disappointment, even failure. As one experienced executive noted wryly, "You can easily pay out $20 to $50 million and end with nothing, or, worse, bring your operations to a screeching halt."

- There are a number of identifiable managerial strategies and skills that enable companies to cope with the challenges inherent in this extraordinary paradox: outsiders are now involved in some of the most important, intimate, and vulnerable aspects of the business. This paradox and those strategies are the subject of this book.

The Plan of the Book

Our emphasis is on managerial strategies for collaborating with outside companies who handle information systems development and information technology management. We also explore the often unexpected challenges faced by outsourcers when naïve client executives believe that they can just "turn it over" to the experienced vendors of their choice. (Naïve outsourcers will sometimes think this kind of control will make their job easier. They soon find out that for the system to succeed in implementation, they need the active participation and involvement of the business and its end users.)

Our examples underscore what line managers must do to work collaboratively with outsourcers so their contribution enhances the performance of business units. We also emphasize the strategies by which line managers can incorporate computer-based information systems into their arsenal of day-to-day working tools for improving performance. All of this depends on line business managers learning how to play a key role in how systems get designed and function, learning their potential, and becoming comfortable with their use. There is no better testing ground for executives to learn about partnering than in situations where there is instability, change, and innovation.

Chapter 2 brings together surveys and cases that underscore the problems faced by companies and their managers when parts or all of their information systems get outsourced. Our first "pass" at providing answers to these problems is incorporated in Chapter 3. The emphasis is on new, risk-averse ways of strategically approaching the development of information systems and dispelling the most common myths in the field. Chapter 4 focuses on aiding managers in thinking through ("scope" is the jargon) how best to approach improving or developing a new information system. Chapter 5 provides very specific techniques and criteria for selecting an outsource contractor and, conversely, knowing which to avoid. The often unanticipated problems associated with subcontractors are described in Chapter 6.

Outsourced ongoing operations provide a different set of challenges than using contractors to develop a new or modified system. How client/inside users can be assured that their objectives are being met—and customer needs satisfied—is the subject of a number of cases in Chapter 7. The more complete, extended case studies of *successful* outsourcing that grow out of the studies that form the background of this book are in Chapters 8 to 11. Chapter 8 is an overview; Chapter 9 is based on a major data warehouse project in one of America's largest and most successful specialty retailers; Chapter 10 involves the first introduction of imaging technology in a very profitable division of what is now a huge financial services company. Here an operations manager spearheaded the effort and the outsourcer was also the provider of hardware as well as software. The last case, described in Chapter 11, involved a European telecom seeking an information systems solution to a costly internal problem.

Chapters 12, 13, and 14 offer an inside look at the frequently misunderstood dynamics of new systems development projects. The torturous path we describe underscores all the uncertainties that lead to the many departures from the carefully outlined original plan.

Understanding the tough challenges associated with software development helps client managers become more realistic in terms of what to expect and when and where their inputs are essential. Chapter 14 explains the counter-intuitive finding: often, under the right circumstances, near project failure is the precursor to creative, effective systems. Chapter 15 outlines the steps required to effectively implement a new system to avoid wasting a new resource. Chapter 16, with many examples, explores a major theme: the critical role of the line manager/user. Outsourcing, badly handled, can discourage managers from becoming more computer literate at the very time that these systems are becoming central to their jobs. The last chapter of the book is a general overview of our work and compares information system expertise with how companies have handled other "new" specialization in the past.

The Tough Dilemmas:
Why the Obvious Is So Difficult

Managers involved in the outsourcing of information technology rarely have the luxury of stepping back from the fray to ask some basic questions about this very challenging and often daunting process. As they will learn, few business decisions are simultaneously both obvious and trouble free. A good place to begin is by placing outsourcing in a broader perspective.

The New Automation: A Focus on Coordination, Systems, and Service

Companies have been automating for many decades: moving components in manufacturing from one process to another without human intervention. Much newer is "white-collar" automation: getting continuity in the movement of data and paper flows. The focus of what is called the Second Industrial Revolution is much more on facilitating decision making, innovation, and service (in contrast to manufacturing efficiency). The goals are the same: decreasing the need for human intervention, attaining faster response time, and reducing internal inconsistencies. The Caterpillar Company provides a typical example:

> We're using the latest advances in information technology to benefit customers . . . we're linked electronically with 1,300 of our suppliers—handling purchasing orders, releases, shipping schedules and invoices without paper. . . . Our vision includes a global parts search, machine prognostics and diagnostics via satellite. . . . Or we can give field service technicians the tools to tap into our parts support system from a service truck.[1]

Thus, as companies came "under the gun" (or confronted Asian competitors) in the high pressure, competitive environment of the 1980s, they turned to reorganization. The buzzword was "reengineering." They sought new workflow systems that ignored traditional functional or departmental boundaries. The objective: smooth, uninterrupted flows that assure efficiency, service, and quality.

The emphasis on operating capability and processes such as order fulfillment, new product development, and integrated supply chains means an emphasis on *data processing and information flows*, the work of computers. The much-heralded strategic emphasis on *core competencies* essentially rests on critical processes, not functional specialization.

Outsourcers to the Rescue

Ironically and paradoxically, just as companies discover that operations and service and the processes underlying them are integral to their core competency, they decide to outsource the supporting technology. But the explanation is widely known—the soaring costs and complexity and rapid changes characteristic of information technology. Senior management has watched its technology costs soar exponentially over the past decade.[2] There has been a proliferation of new hardware and software, rapid obsolescence, and a cacophony of new systems, many of which have compatibility problems. Unlike the more traditional business functions of marketing and production, the nuances of contemporary information technology represent a formidable intellectual challenge to most managers. They suffer grave doubts when it comes time to assess the cost/benefit relationships underlying technology budgets.

It is hardly surprising that companies turn outside to specialized information technology service providers. Many of these appear to offer the convenience of "one-stop" purchasing: predictable costs. And, of course, there is the side benefit that the executives don't have to manage (and therefore understand) the complexities of these arcane, esoteric, ever-changing technologies.

A Plus for the Bottom Line

For many executives, IT services are excellent candidates for outsourcing. They are viewed as a utility, a kind of composite of telephone service and transaction processor. In addition, there can be a kind of vicious (or benign, depending on your point of view) cycle operating. Downsizing and restructuring often cut deep into IT staffs and make new development initiatives (often intended to further increase labor savings) difficult to handle internally. Outsourcing has become a means for corporations to cut personnel but still get the job done. And, for financial reporting purposes, it can be impressive to show lower head counts and a smaller asset base denominator for calculating profitability. These manipulations are not insignificant motivations for going outside.

Avoiding Some Tough Political Decisions. Mergers often create politically sensitive dilemmas about integrating a company's diversity of IT groups. A seemingly simple way to deal with the issues is to outsource most of the IT function, thus eliminating the need to negotiate which company's staffs or systems get retained or which get axed.

Why the Obvious Really Is Difficult

Not surprisingly, for most senior management today, outsourcing information technologies seems a "no brainer," an easy decision. They take comfort in the assumption that their contractors will then bear the burden of developing new computer systems and keeping up with the blistering rate of technological change. A typical senior executive's expectations for outsourcing are these (as described in a recent business news story based on an interview of Merrill Lynch's manager of technology for its corporate and institutional client group):

> (He) hires companies like. . . . [well known outsourcers] . . . that he says can tightly define a goal, firgure out what technology is needed to achieve it and execute the project crisply.[3]

What is overlooked in this comforting reliance solely on the outsiders professional knowledge and skill is that building new systems is not just a technical job for systems professionals, but one for the business to reconceive its way of managing work, customer relations, and management information.

Companies also outsource the more routine aspects of their information technology (e.g., operating and maintaining computer systems, internal communications, networks, and call centers). Vendor costs appear lower and their professional expertise higher than when the work is done inside. It doesn't appear that different from using an external "utility" to provide communication services or a payroll service vendor to calculate employee earnings and produce checks. These are poor analogies, however. This kind of outsourcing is profoundly different from what most companies have done in the past when they have turned to outside vendors.

As countless management experts have observed, information is the lifeblood of every organization. Core business functions may be totally dependent on these outsourced systems. In many companies (Wal-Mart is always given as an example), integrated, cross-functional systems are proprietary crown jewels. Automation and telecommunications are often vital components of the most critical work of the corporation: marketing, production, and service. Increasingly, hard driving companies want these functions tightly interconnected—via their information systems, of course! Who gets what data, when, and in what form also has a profound impact on executive decision making.

Whoever controls communications linkages, data and transaction processing, as well as decision and service support functions directly affects the core operations of any business. There is no way of erecting an impervious wall separating these "non-core" activities from the critical managerial and operating processes: how work gets done, decisions get made, and the customer gets service and satisfaction.

Tempting as it may be, management can't delegate its responsibilities. Outsourcing in this arena is by no stretch of the imagination similar to outsourcing mundane, peripheral business functions. And it is very naïve, indeed, to believe that few internal human resources will be needed. As we will see later, a substantial amount of a company's best business and line managers are required if these systems are to perform in ways that advance the company's strategy.

Caveat Emptor: Many New Information System Projects Fail

Equally compelling concerns should arise when clients contemplate the rate of failure of new system development projects. Several confidential consultant reports suggest that a minority of these projects meet their schedule and cost goals and a large proportion don't deliver the functionality that had been expected by users.

- Roughly speaking, it is estimated that almost a third of computer application projects get canceled before completion. More than half cost more than double their original estimates. In large companies less than 10% are completed on time and within budget. And, of those completed, the systems have less than half the originally proposed features and functions.[4]

- Three-quarters of all large systems are "operating failures" that either do not function as intended or are not used at all.[5]

As noted in Chapter 1, many companies are profoundly dissatisfied with their outsourced information systems.

Some Examples of the Bad News

Everyone is now familiar with the phrase, "Our systems are down so we can't. . . ." Most companies are almost as dependent on their hardware and software as they are on electric power. And, of course, it isn't just breakdowns or "bugs"—the most visible kind of problems—that impact operation. More insidious are the persisting disabilities created by new systems that fail to perform effectively. The following example is an extreme case because the problem was so publicly visible.

Greyhound. The Greyhound Bus Company funded an expensive new computerized ticketing system. When implemented, it was responsible for a precipitous drop in earnings at Greyhound as well as enormous customer disapproval:

> The original software, developed by an outside company, was a disaster. Learning to use it required 40 hours of training. . . . Because its data bank didn't include all Greyhound destinations, clerks sometimes had to haul out old log books and plot journeys by hand. . . . When the new software was installed at 50 locations, computer terminals began to freeze up unpredictably. . . . [The centralized computers] were so swamped that, on some days, they took as long as 45 seconds to respond to a single key stroke and five minutes to print a ticket (and) agents were writing tickets manually. For days, passengers missed connections, were separated from their luggage and left to sleep in terminals overnight.[6]

Andersen Consulting versus UOP. Given their mutual embarrassment, contractor and clients usually can be reluctant to have their disagreements made public even when costly problems have occurred. When UOP believed it had been wronged by Andersen Consulting, UOP sued for $100 million, thus allowing the kind of problem that is usually hidden from public view to become public.[7] UOP was charging that Andersen failed to deliver systems that would work and their charges were escalating:

[UOP] figured the job would cost 15 million. That was steep . . . but Andersen promised that the new system would help UOP "respond to customer needs 50% faster." . . . In its suit, filed in March 1995, [UOP] says it paid Andersen Consulting 8 million in fees for unusable computer systems that will cost "at least 21 million" to salvage. . . . [One of the two new systems] took longer to use than the old one it was supposed to replace. . . . In its statement, Andersen notes that "no specific deliverables," such as cost or time for completion, were set forth in its contract with UOP.[8]

The following are a few other well-known examples.

Denver's New Airport. There was wide publicity given to the costs incurred by the new state-of-the-art Denver airport that endured embarrassing delays when the baggage system's innovative technology failed to function properly.

The London Stock Exchange. Many ambitious new systems fail to function totally and must be abandoned. Europeans were surprised, however, when the London Stock Exchange scrapped six years of work and wrote off $600 million when it shut down its Taurus project (to computerize settlements).[9]

Government. In the United States, there are frequent press references to the embarrassing multibillion-dollar failures of both the FAA and the IRS as they have repeatedly funded new information systems. Recently, California wrote off a failing $100 million, four-year investment in a new information system, its State Automated Child Support System to track "deadbeat" fathers.[10] Several years ago, New Jersey funded an impressive new Department of Motor Vehicle system to handle registration, licensing, and record keeping of traffic offenses. The new system stumbled when it could not cope with the normal volume of throughput. (Obviously, and perhaps regrettably, public and quasi-public organization failures get known; corporate debacles are less frequently publicized.)

Information Technology: The Most Challenging Change Management Faces

In many applications there is a race between the rapidly evolving computer and communications technologies and the growing and changing corporate demands for information systems. This has an impact not only on outsourced operations, but also new systems development. Major systems integration projects can take five to ten years to develop and fully implement; during that time many of the major parameters on which the system was predicated may well have changed profoundly. In effect, an unwary client can end up looking like one of the hard-panting dogs at a greyhound track chasing the lifeless target that will never be within its grasp.

The huge software programs that underlie the performance of most new information systems are extraordinarily complex (often involving millions of lines of code), with a high degree of probability of having embedded "bugs." These programs are both fragile and challenging to develop as well as frustrating to maintain. Here is an example of how much effort is required to implement what seems like a modest systems requirement:

> [The CEO of a major insurance company]: Our customers are a mobile group; they move once every three years. And they didn't enjoy having to call each and every one of our lines of business to register the same change of address. I ordered that changed. . . . I was shocked when it took us a full year and a half to get the necessary systems and processes lined up so that a person could call any of our lines of business to report an address change, and have it posted immediately in other businesses as well.[11]

Given the inherent complexity and continuing turbulence in both the technology and management requirements of these programs, it is not surprising that their failure rate is so high. The only surprise is the slight client management attention to the problem.

Unrealistic Management Expectations: The Myths and Dilemmas of Outsourcing

Our studies suggest that the expectations and behavior of the user/customer are as critical to the success of the development project as the skills and resources of the contractor, if not more so. In fact, many customers are their own worst enemies. Success for a customer or user of outsourcing depends on the ability of managers to cope with a number of seeming contradictions and dilemmas. Executives must learn how to avoid the strong temptation to pretend that simple, static, rule-based solutions exist.

While the technology itself is obviously new, it is reassuring (and deceptive) to believe that there is little new to learn about managing it; the old rules should still apply. The simple, appealing commonsense principles of management aren't a particularly useful guide in managing these new technologies. (And, of course, outsourcer managers need to sensitize themselves to these erroneous client "maps" of their world.) Regrettably, those old principles have spawned a number of myths that have become security blankets for many executives when they outsource new systems development.

The Technology Myth. Developing new technology has become relatively easy—so it is believed. (Americans' culture-based optimism has received an enormous boost from this generation's experience with the incredible dynamism of modern technology.) It is as if there was real truth in the boast: "We do the difficult immediately but it will take us a little longer to do the impossible." It is hard not to be awed by technologists who run real-time experiments on the Martian surface and clone mammals. Almost every day the business press describes a remarkable new product or process. Yet new enterprise-wide systems, particularly large ones that seek to integrate several previously independent business functions or handle an enormous number and variety of transactions can be extraordinarily difficult to develop and implement (or modify). The understandable enthusiasm of the seller (i.e., the outsource contractor) and the eagerness of the buyer (i.e., the client) to shift responsibility to a competent, responsible outsider often mask these well-documented hazards.

The Prescient Client Myth. Any sensible client for a new system, it is believed, knows what they want and can spell out in very objective detail their performance requirements. These often get incorporated into the familiar request for proposal (RFP), and contractors will vigorously compete to determine who will get the contract to do what the client feels has been meticulously defined.

In fact, most clients, at least at the outset, cannot know, much less make explicit, all their needs and requirements. Important constraints and requirements are often buried deep in the bowels of the organization and the memories of experienced "worker bees." There is a torturous path leading from initial needs and objectives analyses to the eventual configuration of an operating system. Most users learn some of what they need and want only *after* they see working prototypes and learn to adapt their potential.

The Project Management Myth. Starting with these requirements, this myth asserts, there is a clear straight road for the systems integrator: translating those requirements into software code. Thus, effective project management will be almost synonymous with the formal procedures of project management. Good planning and controls (checkpoints and such) are obviously essential. But managers who expect their plans to predict future outcomes are naïve. Effective systems development is synonymous with creative problem solving of *unanticipated crises and demands*. Good controls must be balanced with a significant amount of flexibility in the development process that provides opportunities for the client and the outsourcer to experiment and learn both from the process and each other.

All of this is in sharp contrast to the naïve belief that software development is a straightforward process of translating clear requirements into machine language.

The Contract as Complete Guarantee Myth. A well-written contract is reassurance that the client's needs will be satisfied—or the client's money back, maybe with interest. It should contain the unambiguous specifications for the new system, meticulously detailed concerning performance, price, and schedule. The contract provides the client with the major lever to ensure that the contractor will produce the desired system. After all, the client can always "hold their feet to the fire" if problems occur, or so it is believed.

Carefully crafted contracts do, of course, play an important role in outsourcing, but experienced managers know their limitations and the importance of mutual adaptation to omissions, unanticipated project-threatening obstacles, new opportunities, and new requirements that emerge during the development process. Usually the contractor can find any number of client-initiated changes, failures, or omissions to justify (legally) shortfalls in performance or cost increases.

The Prestigious Contractor/Outsourcer Myth. In the comfortable "good old days," many executives bought from Big Blue (IBM) as a risk-averse strategy. If problems occurred, they couldn't be blamed for buying an off-brand or the wrong technology. Many of those same executives adopt the same strategy by outsourcing their new systems or applications development work to a Big Blue equivalent, the best name brands. The "myth" then assures them that they can step back, relax, and let the outsider take responsibility for fulfilling their requirements. These same clients also buy into the marketing assurance that an experienced contractor "knows your business almost as well as you do," particularly if they have worked in the same industry.

Unfortunately, reputation doesn't guarantee performance in developing new information technology.[12] A prestigious contractor (however "deep" their pockets) cannot guarantee success. As later chapters will describe, even the best often overstate their competencies—and the client's likely savings—misconstrue or fail to fully comprehend their client's requirements, use inexperienced personnel, and shortcut testing to meet unrealistic schedules. There are also many cases in which excellent vendors walk away from projects. And the ability to field large numbers of bodies may not help, but hinder. Small numbers of excellent staff accomplish much more than hundreds of fresh-out-of-school programmers. An outsider rarely, if ever, can comprehend all the nuances of operations or the requirements of innovative strategies.

It is comforting to assume that all the frustrations of the development project get borne by the contractor, and that all the client needs to do is play a largely oversight or even adversarial role. But playing the passive partner in the venture actually exposes the client to much more risk and cost as well as the possibility of failure.

The Easy Teamwork Myth.   Today's executive recognizes the importance of teamwork. But there is widespread underestimation of the need for continuing intimate exchange, trade-off, coordination, and communication in systems development projects. Some of the most successful software firms have learned that truly great software is created by a single programmer. They never want teams larger than seven or eight. But major new systems projects often employ large numbers of programmers. And increasingly these projects involve geographically and organizationally dispersed professionals and managers. (Often "team" members will be in different time zones or overseas.) There are no easy answers to managing without physically proximate teams, although new technologies facilitate "virtual" organization.

The Myth of Choosing Centralization or Decentralization.   Systems performance, data security, and integrity all require a great deal of centralized control of information technologies (when outsourced and left in the hands of the contractor). But modern PC-based systems allow for a great deal of line manager initiative in developing innovative solutions for day-to-day operating problems and overcoming costly inefficiencies in the larger systems they must use. (Surprisingly, as later chapters document, without this business manager involvement and initiative, the systems themselves will be in trouble; efficiency and service suffer.)

Management strategies for technology development must balance the strong pressures for increasing centralization with the need for reasonable decentralization. As in other areas of business strategy, this balancing act has never been easy; companies have usually preferred the "excesses" of going all one way.

The Myth That Partnering Is Partnering.   Most companies have made great strides in learning how to partner with a select group of vendors, sharing information and providing some guarantees. But these partnerships understate the challenges inherent in outsourcing information systems. They still emphasize a defined, structured type of model:

1. Decide what you want and put it unambiguously in a RFP and then a contract.
2. Select a good partner-contractor to do the work.
3. Check up and pay for performance.
4. When performance doesn't meet expectations, get a refund and change partners.

Outsourcing systems development is more complex. What users need will change in any dynamic business environment and as they experience a new system's capabilities and learn of still newer technological resources. And it is by no means easy to change partners.

Reprise

There is no simple risk-avoidance strategy. Management first has to give up a great deal of wishful thinking—what we have termed myths—about the process of outsourcing these complex technologies.

So much of any system is invisible and untouchable, and the millions of coded instructions, even with the most careful programming, are fertile ground for small but disastrous errors. Too many customers for outsourcing abdicate their responsibilities. The reasons are not complex; constantly changing technologies are intimidating. Customers blithely presume that a good contract guarantees the outsider will do "everything." They also assume that very limited internal technical human resources will be required.

Instead of relaxing when all the responsibility for making these complex technologies work effectively has been placed on the capable shoulders of the outsider, managers must engage in a very demanding and more involved style of partnering.[13] Outsourcers who have experienced clients who won't sign off on completed systems and complain bitterly that "It's not what we expected" have as much to gain from the intensive partnering we will be describing as their clients.

The following chapters provide specific guidance in planning for information systems development and operation: scoping a project, selecting appropriate outsourcers, and working with them during the development and implementation stages. We also look critically at the dynamics of the relationship between outsourcers handling ongoing operations and their clients. The longer cases contained in Chapters 9 to 11 demonstrate the extraordinary gains to be achieved in new systems that are the product of effective partnering. In these cases, the business managers/users played critical roles in both the early planning and actual development stages. Their contribution and involvement led to automation that increased cost effectiveness, as well as service, by factors of 100% or more.

The next chapter explores the best management strategies and practices for avoiding the most frequent blunders in outsourcing information systems.

Outsourcing Strategies:
Avoiding the Most Frequent Blunders

When planning to outsource information technology, senior management must have a strategy informed by the success and failure of other companies. Based on projects we personally observed as well as those described by others, we have a short list of strategy blunders to avoid. Here are some of the most frequent mistakes that can doom these important—and often costly—new projects.

Go for the Newest Technology;
Don't Be Left Behind

There is great appeal, even fascination, in selecting state-of-the-art technology. Vendors and outsource contractors find that the newest pathbreaking technology sells. We live in a dynamic world of technology where new is better, or at least presumed to be. And why buy the equivalent of an old model? Particularly when management is playing "catch up," trying to make up for lost time—when it had failed to keep up with the competition in automating its information systems—there are strong psychological pressures to go all the way. The phrase is often used that management is paying for "bragging rights," the ego boost associated with having the newest machine on the block.

Reality: Many of the innovations that senior management finds most attractive are cost "sinks." They take companies down a primrose path of cost overruns and clumsy systems that either don't work for years or work badly. A sensible customer for a new system wants *"state of the market,"* not "state of the art." A conservative outsourcing strategy emphasizes seeking the *best technology that has been proven under varied operating conditions by real-life users.*

> The Federal Aviation Administration followed this simple precept when it decided to use Raytheon as the prime contractor for installing a very sophisticated new system that can handle as many as 1200 planes simultaneously. Raytheon got the contract by proposing to use off-the-shelf computers and to recycle almost 85% of the software (already proven in use in aircraft control systems developed in foreign countries). This outsourcing was a major departure from the Agency's previous emphasis on custom designed systems.[1]

The newest usually means unproven—lots of unknown and even unknowable problems. The history of technology is filled with examples of exciting laboratory breakthroughs that failed to function effectively when confronted with real production and operating settings.[2]

The value of a new system, its effectiveness and contribution, usually depends as much, if not more, on the user's adaptation and application, not the sophistication of the technology. As many experienced executives have learned through trial and error, the most cost-effective systems also reflect a productive partnering relationship between users and technologists.

Don't Be a Wimp; Be a Guinea Pig

There may be some macho thrill associated with being one of the first companies to employ a pathbreaking technology. Vendors for these innovations are likely to provide appealing demonstrations. Never be satisfied with hearing about or observing a new technology under "controlled conditions." A potential customer should be able to see a technology being considered for purchase at work under normal operating conditions: high and ever-changing volume, typical, less-than-perfect employees as operators, problems with "dirty data," and an adverse operating environment.

Buy the Kitchen Sink and Everything Else

Akin to having the newest, executives find it appealing to sponsor truly large (enterprise-wide), fully integrated systems—tying together all the information flows of a company: customer accounts, operations, marketing, accounting, field offices, headquarters.

Reality: Big is rarely better; small is good (usually). One of the authors watched a major insurance company flounder when it outsourced the development of a huge information system to one of the largest and most prestigious outsourcers in the systems business. The outsourcer convinced the company that it could develop a system that would link all of its farflung offices, independent agents as well as sales, policy origination, and customer service. Hundreds of millions were spent before they threw in the towel. The system never worked.

At another international insurance company, a very senior executive was embarrassed when one of his major customers (with operations dispersed around the world) showed him how much business they were doing with his company. Almost the next day, he pronounced this edict: "We will develop an information system that will allow us to access and display all the policies we write for a given corporation regardless of the region in the world or the subsidiary name." Because it was given such a high priority, an outsourcer was found who seemed willing and able to deliver this system. The outsourcer and the insurance company vastly underestimated what was required to integrate the twenty different, diverse, and incompatible accounting and information systems of their regional groups scattered around the world. After several years, very little progress had been made.

Very large projects bring special disabilities; the diseconomies of scale are one. Never mind the complexity of these behemoths—

their size alone multiplies risk. As a highly experienced project manager noted, "Any project that requires over 10,000 person-days of effort exhibits negative economies of scale; it becomes a very high risk project."

Experienced observers believe that a project team of more than fifty people is highly vulnerable to intergroup conflict and poor coordination. Obviously, many projects are going to require large staffs, but clients need to know that the inherent complexity of the task is worsened by the numbers of programmers. These are also the projects most likely to cross time and cultural boundaries as outsourcers seek increased numbers of scarce technical resources.

One senior executive of a major system integrator that provides professional services in the systems field observed wryly: "We find often that when our clients don't really understand their requirements, they simply look for 'Cadillac' solutions. They think that more is better." These clients obviously forget that information systems are also liabilities; costly to maintain as well as develop. They ignore the reality that it will cost 15 to 20% of the original cost *per year* for maintenance alone. Worse yet, when maintainability is not designed in (by the systems developer), this rule-of-thumb figure can skyrocket dramatically.

It is extraordinarily easy (and typical) for both clients and their outsource contractors to underestimate the difficulty of translating the conception of a new system into a robust, easily maintained operating technology. Much too often, both sides discover belatedly that what was agreed to is more difficult than anyone imagined. As they grow larger and more complex, the potential for problems increases exponentially. These large systems are extraordinarily vulnerable; even small problems can cause major dislocations in a company's operations. And truly big projects can take years to complete—five, six, even seven years are not that unusual. Imagine how much technology will have changed at the end of such a period. And what about the client's needs, markets, and operations? Will they stand still? In brief, as many experienced project managers will say, "Beware of grandiosity." It is probably just as difficult to bring together and integrate diverse computer systems as to merge the cultures of diverse companies. (Experienced programmers have observed that they can decipher the unique organizational culture that spawned a new system in its code!)

Experts Always Know Best

Information technologies are becoming more and more complex and dynamic. It is foolish and costly to think a company's management can do better than the specialists. Shift as much as you can to expert outsiders and stick to core competencies.

Reality: Competent outsource contractors can be enormously useful. They often have broad industry-relevant experience and ought to know the potential (and inherent shortcomings) of relevant technologies. But the presumption that the outsider can just jump in and take over is naïve. Every outsourcer, almost by definition, has real limitations in terms of its understanding of any particular business, its inner workings as well as operating and strategic needs.

No outsider really knows the operating dynamics of a specific business even with substantial, relevant industry experience. And it is a profound mistake to expect them to prescribe what is needed. No amount of written and verbal presentations takes the place of continuous involvement of actual users. The outsider can learn a good deal, but that learning must come as real problems and choices present themselves during development and implementation or transition of operations management.

The largest division of a major corporation was outsourcing the development of an important application program. The requirements were specified by IT managers. As is typical, this internal group was acting as a liaison to the outsourcer. In preparing their assessment, the IT group had excluded actual users from any involvement. Among the specifications for the new system was the replication of several hundred user "screens" available to users under their old systems. The outsourcer accepted without question this requirement. It first tried to implement the system as proposed and only after finding it too complex approached the actual users—only to find that they too found the number of screens daunting. The result—the number was reduced to only a dozen screens, each designed with the end users' needs in mind. That change in requirement resulted in enormous savings in development time and targeted a less complex, easier to use and maintain system.

Insiders Obviously Know What They Need

Although the knowledge and needs of users are indispensable in systems planning, past practices and policies can get in the way of creative thinking. As we saw in the previous case, past practices are not always a good guide in the design of a new system.

Line managers, working within their divisional and functional boundaries, are often reluctant to take on policies or practices outside their direct control—thus dampening the broad "integrating" impact that new systems can have in changing the way work gets done or decisions are made. The best planning decisions get made when those who are well informed about technology interact with and challenge those who know their business problems and requirements.

Go for the Perfect Plan

Conventional wisdom is that it pays to make sure that the planning is as close to perfect as human beings can make it. There is so much management rhetoric stressing the importance of waiting to begin until all the planning is complete. Then the development can progress smoothly to completion.

Reality: No plans are complete or are able to foresee every contingency (or even most). It is better to start with a general direction and learn as you go along.

The *Wall Street Journal* reported that the Internal Revenue Service has spent $8 billion over the past ten years just in developing a "preliminary" plan for modernizing document processing. They quote a National Research Council report (an organization of the National Academy of Sciences) saying that this planning effort has been an almost total failure.[3]

Later chapters will provide many examples of how well-designed plans required major modifications as new systems were under development. The effort to hold tightly to the plan often created horrendous problems.

Buying Pre-owned Systems Software Will Save Time and Money

It is tempting to buy a system that is up and running in the same or a similar industry. Often an outsourcer will have shared the cost of developing the system for one client with the expectation that they will realize bonus returns from selling it to new users. At other times, an outsourcer will use a software company as a subcontractor for a systems development project with some proprietary software that will constitute the core of a new system being developed for a client.

Reality: Pre-owned systems are sometimes no bargain. All too frequently, all parties vastly underestimate the time, effort, and money required to customize or adapt a system for a new client. Thus, adding or subtracting some features in an existing large program may appear rather simple, at least compared to writing an entirely new program. But the real cost comparisons when an IT specialist says that 95% of the program is reusable may not be that obvious and could even be deceptive. That new "small" 5% may be intertwined with many parts of the program that are supposed to remain the same.

The current costly crises associated with introducing what appear to be slight changes in an existing program, the Year 2000 problem, is a good example. The hundreds of billions estimated to "fix" the problem reflect the reality that computer programs are incredibly complex. Their elements have an overwhelming number of interdependencies, some proportion of which are usually unknown and even unknowable *before modifications are undertaken.*

Here are some other reasons to be wary when told it will be relatively simple to recycle and adapt a pre-owned system:

- Often there will have been breakthroughs in hardware and software that this older program doesn't encompass. Newer hardware frequently incorporates more efficient benefits and fixes that in the past had to be designed into custom software. Using pre-used software to do the job can mean you'll be saddled with a clumsier, low-performance solution.

- When the system has been used for some time, there are likely to be a variety of embedded changes, modifications, and "work-arounds" improvised to cope with "bugs" or other problems experienced by users. These are developed after the system is in production (use), and the changes probably don't get back to the vendor.

- Not infrequently, significant gaps exist in the documentation of the code. When rushed (since documentation takes substantial time), programmers often neglect this painful step. To make the transfer more difficult, many of the programmers who knew the original system have probably moved on.

A better alternative to buying or renting a used system is to acquire consulting assistance from those with the knowledge base embodied in these programs. Companies seeking new systems can try to hire those who have experience with the kind of transactions and data flows they wish to automate. Buying knowledge can be a better strategy than buying code.

You Will Only Need a Skeleton Internal IT Staff

Every eighteen months these computer-based technologies go through major changes. And the demands for expert talent are outrunning the supply. No wonder a company feels relieved that the outsourcer will handle these issues and the costly and potentially increasingly obsolete internal staff can be very substantially downsized.

Reality: Increasingly, companies find that they have a substantial need for internal technical staff. Reliable and sophisticated monitoring is essential for outsourcing—performance is rarely obvious and requires continuous surveillance. Technology costs are highly volatile and client-side experts need to challenge outsourcer "accounting." There will always be important projects that should be done inside, working closely with users. Even those shipped outside require internal coordination and inputs.

Beware of shortcuts and no pain solutions. Fast-changing, complex, costly information technologies can be a source of enormous frustration to senior management. Each year brings higher costs and more crises. Thus, it is very tempting to find a topnotch expert outsider who will take the source of the trouble off your hands. The outsourcer's appeal is the promise of increased predictability and regularity in the cost and performance of company information technology. Often the decision is made when management becomes profoundly concerned about some major gap or deficiency in their information systems. After dawdling for years, they now want to take action swiftly. It is comforting to these senior executives to think they are shifting total responsibility for accomplishment to an experienced outsider.

But systems development is inherently complex, prolonged, and painful. Many of the larger projects are among the most frustratingly difficult technology application endeavors with which business is involved. Tempting as it may be to maintain the illusion that the well-qualified outsourcer has time tested routines that guarantee success, a great deal of carefully timed user involvement is required. The "long cuts" with a good deal of trial and error and involvement by business managers and internal IT staff are much more likely to produce a product that facilitates and grows with the business.

Critical Learning Required

New computer-based information systems are much more fragile, vulnerable, trouble-prone, and more challenging to create than most client/buyers recognize. Although almost every organization has moved into the computer age, new programming tools are constantly being developed, and the economy has large numbers of competent suppliers of services and well-trained personnel, creation is still a frustrating, costly, risky business. The risks go up enormously on large projects; they become incredibly high when clients seek state-of-the-art solutions; and they are needlessly multiplied when these clients have unrealistic beliefs about the amount of relevant knowledge possessed by outsiders *and insiders.*

Outsourcers are almost always less expert than they appear, and clients need to have their wholly owned or at least wholly loyal experts to assess the quality and cost of services received. Without substantial inputs and involvement from inside line managers, it is highly unlikely that an outsourced system will meet critical operating needs. But these managers will find it difficult to conceive of the dimensions involved in a truly innovative system when they have not experienced the relevant new (at least to them) technologies.

In the next chapter, we explore this perplexing dilemma that confronts all companies seeking to develop a new information system. Techniques are outlined that will aid management in "scoping" a new project: determining *where* change is needed, *what* information system initiatives are required, and *how* the company should maintain momentum in continuing systems adaptation.

Planning and Preparation

How does an astute management cope with the high risks of failure, the perplexing dilemmas, and the easy seductions endemic to outsourcing information systems? A simplistic answer: with that time-tested, over-the-counter remedy—realism. That could dispel many of the outsourcing myths and illusions. But then would come the tough part: translating realism into specific managerial strategies. Their objective, of course, is increasing the odds of having a successful outsourcing experience.

What are these strategies? Basically, they are the strategies of engagement. Almost every executive knows only too well the costs of a fully self-sufficient in-house IT staff that can build and maintain the systems to exploit new information technologies. The increasingly automatic reaction is disengagement, passing a good share of information system development and operations off to knowledgeable, responsible outsiders.

Many experienced executives react in the opposite way. Before outsourcing, the organization develops the broad outlines of the kind of system it needs. It does this by intense, management-involved reworking of its operations. In this process, the company grows the internal competence to exploit the expertise of outsourcers and new technology.

A Game Plan for Effective Scoping

A company taking this approach to outsourcing begins by putting in place a structure to *scope the project*, asking *where, what,* and *how*.

- *Where* is there a real need for new or improved automation? Where can we gain major improvements in service quality, cost, and/or performance?
- *What* should the new system do?
- *How* should it do it? This is a general idea of what kinds of technologies may be relevant; what kinds of organizational changes are required.

Effective scoping requires a meticulous choreographing of the interrelationships among the three essential components of good information systems planning:

1. Knowledgeable insiders (who know the business strategies, current practices, and, most important, current obstacles to attaining high efficiency, quality, and service).
2. Technical expertise (probably outsiders as well as insiders) who know the technology options.
3. Creative new insights on the part of line managers about the potential for improvement inherent in one or more technology "solutions" (these are a product of interacting with technology experts).

If these are going to work together to produce a sensible plan, senior management must have "gotten religion" by:

- Understanding the profound difficulties and high risks of failure in overly ambitious, large-scale systems and those based on state-of-the-art technologies and taking steps to avoid or ameliorate them.
- Making unambiguous commitments to the costly involvement of their business managers in both developing and monitoring new information systems.

- Sponsoring and supporting internal company efforts to rethink and reconceptualize new workflow systems that will underlie the design and implementation of new information systems. These need to reflect the potential inherent in new information processing technologies.

Get Real: Assessing the Difficulty of Outsourcing

When senior management considers outsourcing information technology, the discussion usually starts with the popular distinction between core and non-core activities. Every day the financial press heralds yet another senior executive who equates improving profitability with the company's willingness to shed one or more "non-core" functions or businesses. As we have already noted, it is now almost a foregone conclusion that top management will decide: "We are not in the business of developing new information systems or data processing or picking new computer technologies and maintaining them."

Increasingly, the trend has turned to selective IT outsourcing as companies learn the problems of doing it wholesale. Selective outsourcing strategies make a distinction between the kinds of outsourcing that can be handed off to an outsider and those that require continuing, intimate involvement.

*Is It "Core?" Can Be the **Wrong** Question*

Unfortunately, the assessment of what is *really* core is often misguided. To be sure, there are some obvious choices. PC and network maintenance are classic service functions that can be handed off to an outsider. These are far from the core of the business; they are out on the periphery, not unlike cafeterias and guard services. Such technology and information services become the proverbial no-brainer when:

- The function can be precisely defined.

- The function is likely to remain relatively fixed (i.e., stable).

- It can be handled uniformly for all or most parts of the organization and across organizational lines (e.g., with distributors, suppliers).

- Management doesn't expect to gain new knowledge from the function for future marketing or product development strategies.

More daunting and complex information systems may also fit this criteria and benefit from the standardization and simplification outsourcing often imposes.

Funds Transfer: A Case for Outsourcing. Systems for handling funds transfer transactions for banks are good candidates for outsourcing. Each transaction must be formatted and handled in the same way, in every branch and division of a bank as well as in any clearinghouse and other banks in the system. This is an activity that can be and is easily outsourced with rather little management involvement before, during, or after the development of any information system. This is not to say that there is no need for ongoing change and improvement in these systems—but the amount of change expected both in designing these systems and in their use is incremental rather than revolutionary.

Leaving aside such highly routine service functions, outsourcing decision making becomes more problematic, as the following high-technology company discovered.

A Medical Systems Company

A start-up medical systems company had developed a breakthrough system for using holography for viewing multiple medical scans (MRI results) as a three-dimensional whole. In taking the product from prototype into mass production, they needed to develop a supporting shell for their technology. They chose to outsource the development of this shell to a vendor experienced in creating imaging systems.

They set parameters and requirements for the outsourcer, but immediately ran into problems. In touring the imaging vendor's operation and reviewing progress, the insider who had designed the original prototype found many problems with the vendor's design and tried to warn company executives. The contractor complained that the company's representative was interfering and blamed delays on the "troublemaker." As a result, the company removed the "troublemaking" engineer from the project.

With limited give-and-take between the vendor and the client team most knowledgeable about the intricacies of the core product, the product missed its launch date and continued to be plagued by incompatibilities. The vendor met the parameters, but the fit between the shell and the core system proved more complex. After many months had elapsed, it was obvious that the contractor was not going to deliver a usable design (thus creating a financial crisis for the client).

Success on the project would have required a great deal of continuous give-and-take between those insiders who had the conceptual insights and had worked on the original conceptualization and those who were developing the prototype. But both client and outsourcer presumed that the project could be neatly compartmentalized and handled autonomously.

The key strategic question for management is: what functions or activities can be handed off to outsiders and which are closely intertwined with the heart of the business? The answer determines the kind and level of managerial involvement that must be anticipated.

An Outsourcing Decision Matrix

To better evaluate the costs and risks associated with these decisions, it is necessary to take into consideration both the scope of the project's interdependencies and the specificity with which it can be defined (see Figure 1). Obviously, the less well defined and more ambiguous the project scope is, the more difficult it will be to shift total responsibility to an outsider. Somewhat less obvious,

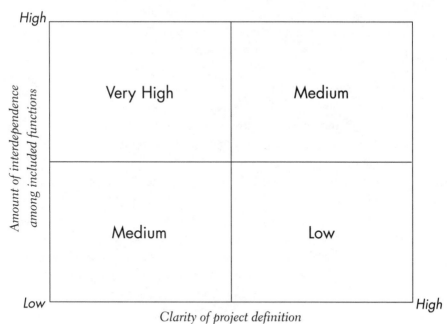

Clarity of project definition

Figure 1.   Outsourcing Matrix: Level of Risk Inherent in the Project

the more the project involves the seamless integration of formerly independent, autonomous functions, the more difficult and risky it will be to outsource.

Where these metrics are high, management must reevaluate its decision to outsource or be prepared to invest very substantially in managerial and professional resources both in the preparation for and conduct of any outsourcing project. The latter means more and higher quality people as well as more internal cost.

The increasingly popular data warehouses are an excellent example of an information system requiring a great deal of user involvement because it is very difficult to define in advance precisely how the system will be employed. Users need to participate actively in the design of these "data banks." They must experiment with what kinds of inventory and marketing queries are now feasible and what additional data would be useful. And then, after the new system is operational, they will want to make changes as products and markets change. (Chapter 9 provides a detailed case of such dynamic interactions between an outsourcer and a sophisticated client.)

Unfortunately, most system software applications—especially those with the most potential return for the organization in terms of new efficiencies, marketing opportunities, and real innovation—are those that are the most difficult to define precisely because they encompass a number of cross-functional interdependencies. They fall in the upper right hand quadrant of the outsourcing matrix shown in Figure 1.

Enterprise-wide information systems run the greatest risk of failure. They have a profound impact on the business practices of most of the key functions and therefore require an extraordinary amount of change. Successful strategies for outsourcing could simply emphasize projects that fall into the low-risk category (i.e., they are highly definable with limited interdependence). Of course, that is increasingly unrealistic.

If the undertaking is more complex, senior management needs to select from an arsenal of strategies that work to reduce uncertainty and cope with the tough challenges introduced when new systems must cross previously sacrosanct jurisdictions and boundaries.

The Where: How to Do Systems Thinking

Regrettably, most managers have never learned to think in systems terms—they were trained in compartmentalized functional terms. A combination of corporate cost accounting and politics usually spawns the familiar "turf" sensitivity, the "silo" approach—looking up and down but not sideways. Most managers need to improve their ability to move away from emphasizing specialization to viewing operations and effective performance in terms of systems, workflows, and processes. Below are some of the concepts that help managers "think systems," not functions.

Reengineering

For some time, systems specialists have used the following framework when looking at a company's work processes:

SIMPLIFY (where possible, routinize tasks).

INTEGRATE (ignore traditional functional boundaries and fine-tune the coordination of tasks required to complete some service or activity to make sure that they really "fit" together).

AUTOMATE (shift as many of these tasks as possible to "automatic" handling, that is, by computer).

The current mantra for those steps is reengineering. Users typically work with system specialists to reconfigure operations that have grown needlessly complex (e.g., with too much variation) and don't flow smoothly. Discontinuities or breaks in the continuous flow of work (materials, paper, and information) are eliminated where possible. Finally, these newly integrated operations get automated, typically by computerization.[1]

The emphasis is on eliminating redundancies (e.g., handling the same data or paper more than once) and coordination (eliminating discontinuities in the flow of work). In many instances the new workflow will represent significant efficiencies because companies historically have emphasized specialization and compartmentalization. In the past, each department or work group is likely to behave in a manner that communicates to others: "We do things our own way—what's easy for us and makes us look good or what we're used to—and what you have to do next to deal with what we send you is your problem, certainly not ours."

Managers shopping for new automation ask themselves questions like these:

- Where are the current workflow bottlenecks; where does work have to be redone, moved back and forth among various "handlers" or stages, or where is there not a smooth, continuous movement (of paper, materials, or data)? Can flows be designed so that paper only gets handled once as it moves from input to output (or, better still, is eliminated completely)?

- What work problems are sources of interpersonal or intergroup arguments and conflict (e.g., over who did what wrong)?

- How can we build in (and automate) the "tacit knowledge," the hard-won experienced judgment exercised by old timers who may no longer be with the organization? (Computer systems can provide what has been called *artificial intelligence* that can be a reasonable replacement for the human decision skills lost with attrition and downsizing.)

- How can relevant "pieces" of data be preserved and then brought together to improve decision quality or speed of response to internal or external customer requests?

- How can interrelated but now separate functions be tied together to improve quality of processing as well as efficiency? (For example, how customer problems will be resolved, how orders will be processed.)

- Where in the flow of work is there too much human intervention; too little? How can a new system focus managerial attention on critical problems where results are beginning to move "out of line"? And how can predictable "disturbances" be handled automatically—that is, without human intervention?

- How can a system (or key subsystems) be developed whose natural boundaries are congruent with an interacting team of employees but also allow a good deal of self-management? Cohesive teams do a better job of working with a system than widely dispersed employees.

- How do we avoid creating systems with perverse incentives (i.e., systems that encourage employees to do things that are injurious to the work of others or the organization)? Here is an example:

  A manager of a customer call center, motivated to reduce costs, decided to reduce the amount of time agents spent on calls. He designed a system that would refer to the back office calls that dealt with inquiries that had been handled by the research area or were in the process of being resolved by a back office department. This strategy backfired as agents took the opportunity to refer all research related inquiries immediately to the back office. Now research was being swamped with often trivial requests, and customers who had formerly received immediate answers to their questions waited for callbacks. What he forgot was that the longer phone time actually satisfied most of these calls and resulted in less work for the costlier back office research function.

- How can we make the system "learn"? A good system will detect error rates and even sources of errors (e.g., subpar quality or service, late deliveries, account errors). Either the system will "propose" changes or those now monitoring the data will have the facts that will provide the basis for considering alternative procedures or corrective actions required of employees (e.g. additional training). A good system will also highlight its own operating deficiencies. Slow response time or inadequate capacity, for example, will create long queues (backlogs) and service delays. (These could require a technological "fix" or an organizational change.)

- How can we assure ourselves that the proposed system is not excessively costly to maintain and enhance? A good system will be easy to enhance—coping with greater volumes and incorporating new functionality.

- How can the company's approach to new systems design take into account future staff development needs? Some relevant examples follow.

  A large Wall Street investment firm decided to outsource the maintenance of its computer systems but not their development. They believed that development was an important learning experience that would "grow" their internal staff's skills, making them more useful for challenging tasks.

  "The ten-year $3 billion outsourcing relationship between Xerox and EDS is structured so that while EDS manages the operational components of the IT infrastructure, Xerox concentrates on new applica-

tion(s). Similarly, Henry Pfendt, the former IT direc-
tor of IT management at Kodak, noted, "Through
outsourcing, it is possible to transform the IT operation from a service deliverer to a broker and facilita-
tor of needed services for business managers."[2]

This brief review of systems analyses suggests a typical way for a
company to begin thinking about its need for new computer-based
automation. That framework can then become the basis for the
hard work of thinking through the basics of a new system.

The What: Working Through the Broad Outlines of a New System

Management must have some notion of what a new system would
do, look like, and accomplish. What are the new interconnections?
How will work and data "flow" in this new processing mode?

Conceive a New System in Its Organizational Context

Managers planning to outsource a new application development
often focus solely on the function or functions to be automated.
These will not operate in a vacuum. As the preceding framework
for thinking through systems emphasizes, as much attention needs
to be given to what changes will be required of those departments
that are inputs to or receive outputs from those functions. They
will have to change their routines and their people will have to
understand and accept these changes—all of which requires managerial efforts.

The users, the line managers who have intimate knowledge of
the business, can make indispensable inputs in creating the performance requirements of a new system. But they also find it difficult
to conceptualize what a system that is not in existence and one
they haven't worked with can and can't do. This explains a very
extraordinary and costly phenomenon. The client refuses to sign
off on the project, claiming that the system fails to meet their

needs. Even when new systems developed by outside contractors meet the requirements specified in the contract (the jargon is that they meet the "scope of work") they can be *rejected by users*. In other words, the client's users got what they thought they needed but it turns out to be not as useful as they had anticipated (or something end users never got the opportunity to review or help define).

Even when seeking to prescribe what they require, experienced line managers make two opposite kinds of errors:

1. They often forget or omit critical steps (because these are taken for granted or done outside their purview). These omissions become major detractions to the new system.

2. They are likely to specify requirements that simply mimic existing procedures and routines; some of which may be redundant or unnecessary. A very experienced contractor, for example, believes that more than 80% of the reports that executives claim they need are really unnecessary. This can make a new system more costly, slower, and more cumbersome than expected.

Both uncertainties—that is, difficulty in providing precise definition and the existence of cross-functional systems—require similar initiatives and commitments. To make user requirements more explicit, users must experience and conceptually comprehend the potential of the new technology. Similarly, most interfaces between functions are not well spelled out. A really effective new system would not be one that simply automated the previous way of passing papers, data, or materials between functions. Interaction and exchange—mutual education—is required between users and outsourcer technical people.

Line Management Defensiveness. It is almost a truism that managers can be defensive. There are thousands of variations of this refrain, "We do fine just as we are; we make our numbers. If there are problems, it is because (fill in the name of another department) can't handle their work properly and we get stuck with their mistakes."

One way of working around this familiar default of denial is to shift the level of discourse. Instead of confronting managers with deficiencies, involve them in meetings with a broader focus. Ask them to be more imaginative and forward looking and deal with broad questions like these:

1. What are the kinds of things that could make for greater customer satisfaction?

2. How can we get closer to our suppliers?

3. What changes would enable us to introduce a new model in less than six months?

Being exposed to "systems thinking," as discussed previously, can stimulate fresh, often creative thinking. One wants managers thinking through work effectiveness in terms of the creation of continuous flows—systems—not functional achievement.

It is often very productive for those responsible for thinking through a new systems project to speak with those on the front lines, the employees closest to the actual operations. More valid data are often forthcoming when these employees are questioned about where the dissatisfactions are (customers, suppliers, other workflow stages); what the greatest time wasters are; or what the things that really frustrate employees are. This approach also has the added advantage of gaining ground-level support and cooperation for a new system (which solves some of their most vexing problems).

How Managers Can Create Their Own New Systems

The following case is an excellent example of how a group of managers were encouraged by their boss to rethink and reengineer the interrelationships among their various functional responsibilities.

Elton was a senior vice president of a major financial services company with a large number of geographically dispersed branch offices. All were dependent for account services on a centralized support division. Concerned about account attrition, Elton decided to launch what he called a "Commitment to Service" program. Its key component was his new policy directive to answer and resolve almost all customer questions or complaints within twenty-four hours.

A new PC-based network connecting back and front offices was the facilitating technology. The projected system would also alert senior management if and when the twenty-four-hour response time was exceeded. That "error" rate, in turn, would direct management's attention to systemic problems.

Elton began a series of meetings with the relevant managers in the branches and their counterparts in the support divisions. The focus was on what needed to be done to make this slogan a reality in practice.

In the early meetings, the branch managers learned the complexity of back office support; why what seemed a simple request could involve substantial complexities before a satisfying answer could be delivered. In fact, both sides learned changes they could make in their procedures that would facilitate a twenty-four-hour response time. And there were some unanticipated surprises. One example: A critical support manager realized that many customer questions could be resolved immediately (without waiting twenty-four hours) if they were directed to the "source" area with the appropriate detailed system information. These calls also often required an interaction with the customer both to find out necessary details and offer explanations—activities the branch staff could not possibly be expected to input into the system. Instead, the manager recommended that the branch use a special hot line to the back office where the questions could be handled and in most cases resolved then and there. In the smaller number of cases where a follow-up action was required, the hot line would input the data into the "Committed to Service" system for their back office operation and tracking of twenty-four-hour turnaround.

Remember that all these systems planning discussions *preceded* the actual design and implementation of the new software. They provided the outsourcer with a number of parameters for the system. Thus, when it came to designing the screens that would appear on the monitors to prompt users, the contractor had the day-to-day work requirements of those users. These had been carefully spelled out in those intensive exploratory meetings.

There is a Catch — The Technology Dilemma

In working through a better, computer-based system, users need more than past experience. A new technology will make dramatic changes in how jobs are performed. Computers will make choices and do calculations that previously had been a burdensome part of the work load. The future job requirements of users depend on the specific capabilities and potential of the new technology.

Realistically, users cannot fully conceive of what it is like to work with a new system without having worked with that system. Thus, an absolutely critical component of these user-based planning meetings is some end-user exposure and comfort level with the software and hardware that will be the underpinnings of the new system.

How New Technology Can Engage the Creativity of Line Managers

Bolstering Line-Manager Capabilities

A successful strategy for outsourcing presupposes an evolutionary, interactive approach to the definition of what is expected and what is to be done. This has to grow out of a dialogue between technology experts and managers and staff with a deep knowledge of the organization's current processes, customers, and their strengths and weaknesses.

Outside resources can help initiate this process, acting as promoters and instigators in the process of reevaluating the way things are done. This could be a "team" that involves one key manager from within, who works in partnership with an outsider. In the very successful data warehousing case in Chapter 9, the client chose a consultant who had a strong general knowledge of its business as well as the technological options available.

Site Visits

There is another excellent technique: seeing what other companies (or divisions) have done with similar automation. Managers are often reluctant to arrange to visit and speak with competitors or companies in other industries who may be utilizing technology similar to what they are considering. This is a very costly and foolish failure.

Often (obviously not always), managers who have been successful in implementing a new system enthusiastically show it to interested outsiders (who can appreciate what they have accomplished). In fact, the amount of openness of other company managers to "peer visits" usually comes as a surprise to those who first try them. Such site visits must include contacts with lower-level personnel who have actually lived with the advantages (and shortcomings) of the new system and the outsourcer. Patient interviewing, with lots of listening, can provide many ideas as to what works and what doesn't, what were the unforeseen problems, and how and with whom they might approach the next system development or outsourcing initiative — based on their previous experience. When well handled, such visitations provide superb and inexpensive consulting from those who have "been there, seen that, done that."

Users Must be Technologically Sophisticated. The highly successful outsourcing examples described in Chapters 9, 10 and 11 illustrate why it is no longer possible for executives to run away from what they perceive as impenetrable technology. Computer-based systems are too important in day-to-day operations and managerial decision making to ignore.

For managers whose experience is limited to a mainframe culture, this represents a profound change in perspective. They were used to tossing their requirements over the transom to an IS department and then waiting patiently or impatiently for something to happen. Rarely was there an opportunity for constructive exchanges between line and staff support.

Successful companies have demonstrated that technically naïve managers, who are not intimated by the jargon and complexity of contemporary hardware and software, can learn enough about the critical dimensions of new systems to make intelligent technology choices. (Many of those who don't are being intellectually lazy.) They've also learned that the design and operation of new computer-based systems get planned best in a learning mode. That is, the conception of "what we need" grows out of continuing exchanges between those who know the business intimately and those who have a feel for the potential of new technologies.

For the exchange between line or business user and staff or technical expert to be productive, line managers must have extended themselves to learn the basics of these new technologies. There are two subtle reasons for this:

1. Often the technology specialist will misinterpret questions being asked or make trade-offs (within the parameters and requirements set forth) that nevertheless have significant consequences for the user. Line managers need to question and challenge to determine what is really feasible (or when, at best, something can only be accomplished at a very high cost or conceivably high risk of failure).

2. The real value of most of these new information systems is only realized when the line manager has a comfortable understanding of the technology. He or she can then add a variety of improvisations to adapt and fine-tune the system to new business needs and market changes.

Understanding doesn't mean knowing how to write code or assemble or take apart the "black boxes." It is feeling comfortable with using the technology as a day-to-day working tool to get everyday business accomplished as well as being able to create new applications.

Leveraging the Potentials of Client/Server Technology

The learning and hands-on approach to developing new systems has been greatly advanced by client/server technologies. These make it easier for business line managers to take an entrepreneurial role. Business managers are learning to use these "front-end" systems to provide continuous feedback about operations and market performance. This information can then be employed further to modify and refine the system to meet the newly updated knowledge base of sophisticated users.

Avoiding User Errors

Knowledge about how the technology functions has other long-run benefits. Involvement with development helps users appreciate the vulnerability as well as the adaptability of these new systems. Naïve users can make destructive errors.

> Boeing had installed a new computer system, but employees were contributing to its malfunctioning. They had little understanding of the system, one of whose features had been designed to avoid the Year 2000 problem. When people typed in "97" (for the year designation) they would be prompted for two more digits. Many simply retyped "97." This caused the computer to analyze parts requirements for the year 9797![3]

They can also make naïve demands. In one large service organization, managers could never understand why the changes they made in their customer offerings were not implemented the next day in the computer's readouts.

Implications for Contractor Selection

The next chapter explores many of the nuances of selecting and contracting with outsourcers. But there are some relevant implications that relate to user-involved planning strategies.

With client/server usage growing rapidly, in part at the expense of the less flexible monolithic mainframe systems, it becomes vital to know whether a potential outsourcer views this technology in ways consistent with an educated, involved user. The contractor must be willing and able to budget project time for experimentation and learning by doing. (Of course, the client has to contribute the time and cost of key "top-of-the-line" users and supporting IS staff). Forward-looking companies should want contractors who perceive this technology and their role as one of

- Educating the line manager/user in becoming better informed about the potential (and limitations) of such systems. Such on-the-job training facilitates their becoming an equal partner in establishing the parameters of any new systems development. (Not surprisingly, this may not be a welcome bonus to some potential contractors.)

- Facilitating line management input in creating new systems and processes that can be continuously adapted as new information is received and processed or as the market and customers change.

- Learning from sophisticated business insiders the kinds of management information these new systems can throw off, almost as a free good, to provide ongoing measurement and feedback on the effectiveness of customer relations programs, new marketing, quality enhancement initiatives, and the like.

The outsourcer in a client/server environment should view the system they will be developing and/or operating as being evolutionary, a work in progress that serves strategic as well as tactical needs of the client's business managers.

The following case of a disappointed user who has shared experiences with other managers in the same industry provides a description of an outsourcer with a major share of the outsourced work in one critical arena. (The example is outsourcing information-processing operations, a so-called third-party processor.)

The outsourcers that many companies in our industry use seem little interested in reflecting the unique needs of any new customers they acquire. They ignore the special features of their clients' internal systems (that must coordinate with the outsourcer's data banks). Thus, when a new customer is acquired, their data files are absorbed into the vendor's system without any attention to inconsistencies that may create processing problems within the client organization. As a result, their clients have to absorb a number of embarrassing operating problems when the outsourcer goes on line with the client's customer files. Over time, these do get worked through. But they put us through a lot of bad times until we could make the proper internal changes or get them to change in order to get the required compatibility in their and our systems.

Some client needs are less sensitive to vendor inflexibility. The economies of scale give these outsourcers the experience and technology to be effective in their major tasks. As long as these requirements remain relatively unchanged, the client is satisfied.

The Elements of a Client-Based Planning Strategy

When there is substantial interdependence between functions (i.e., they require a great deal of real time for mutual adjustment), outsourcing is extremely difficult. A great deal of cooperation and interaction between the contractor and business line manager/ users within the client's organization will be required. (These demands usually far exceed the typical client's expectations.)

- These exchanges need to begin even before a new technology is chosen and a contractor is hired.

- In scoping a new system, there is no way to go directly from how people now work or what they say they want to future design. The phrase "paving cowpaths" captures the fallacy of automating clumsy, needlessly complex ways of working.

- In working through the "scoping" of a new system, managers can establish the core of outsourcing partnering. It then becomes the underpinning of a well-thought-through strategy for handling any new systems development.

- When done well, insiders (often users, sometimes but not always collaborating with internal IS or IT staff) assess their systems requirements. The objective is to find better ways that will depart from the well-worn "cowpaths." By ignoring traditional organization compartments and functions, they can then create workflows that lend themselves to automation.

- These analyses often become more fruitful with the stimulation of the outsider, the potential outsourcer, who exposes both managers and employees to the potential of new automation for information flows. Good contractors, even before a contractual relationship, can become very useful coaches and mentors. Also, as previously noted, site visits can be an invaluable strategy.

- Astute managers expect there will be *dual learning ladders*. Just as their managers' knowledge of what they want will evolve with growing exposure to a new system's capabilities, the outsourcer's knowledge of business needs should continue to grow as they interact with user/managers. Neither should assume their initial objectives and designs will be the last word.

Plan and Execute or Execute and Then Plan

Making intelligent systems design choices obviously requires thoughtful analysis, some of which ought to take place before any discussions with vendors or contractors. But many planning decisions need to get made after the fact. That is, the client decides what they need and want after getting hands-on experience with a new system actually in operation. (Realistically, that means users can experience prototypes or parts of a new system.)

It is most unlikely that devoting adequate time to advance planning will assure the perfect system. There is a big distinction between seeing something on paper and actually using it under everyday and *changing* working conditions. Wise executives expect their new systems to keep evolving with changing business needs and increasing management exposure to the potential of this new information and data source. Thus, it becomes important to plan for systems that will be both changeable and maintainable without undue cost. (Often these kinds of life-cycle considerations are ignored or minimized in setting objectives with an outsourcer. It is not unusual to find companies paying extravagant sums for annual maintenance and change orders.)

Clients always need to emphasize their requirement for the kind of system that is easy and inexpensive to troubleshoot or change as needs or circumstances change. Those characteristics may be more important than how well the system functions initially.

One of the most obvious advantages of the increasingly popular decision support systems, such as data warehouses, is that business managers don't have to think of all of the things they are going to want to learn from a new system in advance. The system can evolve as the manager recognizes new needs; flexibility enables the system to *learn* (and be adaptive to the manager's needs). This is in sharp contrast to traditional computer systems to which line managers had to adapt.[4]

In this dynamic world, the last assumption sensible managers should make is that their required information and data processing is going to remain fixed for any reasonable length of time. Wise executives put aside what may be strong temptations to be at the cutting edge of technology—a very high risk strategy. Similarly, they refrain from the temptation to do everything all at once, to contract for a truly big system that will integrate all aspects of the business.

The toughest information systems to outsource are those that involve highly interdependent functions in the client's organization. Strategies for managing this interdependence emphasize ways to involve and get participation (ownership and creativity) from the client. This does not mean the IT client sponsor, but the real users of the system—managers and end users.

Whether expected performance is realized depends fundamentally on the knowledge, confidence, and contribution of internal line managers. These business managers and their staffs, not the outsourcer, should make the important, tough work-design choices.

There is keen competition for new business among many experienced information systems and technology contractors and they are skilled in making proposals. Experienced insiders have learned to take advantage of this competitive environment and see through glib sales promises when selecting the right vendor. Understanding what a "good" contract will and won't do is one of the most critical requirements for obtaining a new system that will meet user performance needs. This is the subject of the next chapter.

Selecting the Right Outsourcer:
Why Contracts Are No Guarantee

Not surprisingly, the popularity of outsourcing information technology has increased the number of well-qualified, experienced contractors. Clients can select vendors from some of Europe and America's foremost technology companies, the Big Six accounting firms, and literally thousands of other specialized software development companies. There is no shortage of competence. But a wide range of choices means that managers must develop their ability to decide which vendor will be best for their unique project or the organizational context of outsourced operations.

When management decision skills are sound, contractor selection can make an important contribution to the conception and design of the technology and add immeasurably to developing managers and staff. There can be subtle but significant differences among even the most successful outsourcers in terms of their ability to provide these returns.

An appealing, conservative selection strategy is to opt for one of the major firms. They have the proverbial deep pockets should the project get in trouble, and they encompass a number of talented people and broad experience. The catch, so to speak, is that the project's eventual success depends a great deal on the unique abilities of the senior people designated to manage the contract. And there is no guarantee that a big name firm will necessarily furnish superb talent on a sustained basis.

Selecting a contractor and designing the contract are inextricable. A client may gain a certain amount of illusory security by believing that a carefully crafted contract will assure satisfactory results (or fair compensation). Not true, as we will see.

- Many of these new or changed systems will be so essential to the business that the company needs to do everything in its power to seek to avoid failure.

- Client expectations and contractor promises are often so unrealistic that it is highly unlikely that the results will be satisfactory—no matter what the contract says.

- It is rare for a contract to provide complete protection. During the life of the development project many unanticipated changes and client "deficiencies" will surface. Not always, of course, but usually both the inputs and volume specifications promised by the client and the performance specifications promised by the outsourcer are riddled with ambiguities. These enable the contractor to claim, quite legitimately, that it has met the requirements it promised even when the client disagrees.

Much more important than promises and guarantees are the motivation and capabilities of the outsourcer and the quality of the partnership that evolves. Thus, contractor choice is not a simple process of comparing bids from the major players.

This chapter details the critical and often neglected steps that are useful in selecting a contractor as well as some ways of making contracts more dynamic.

Caution: The First Step May Be the Wrong Step

Too often, after deciding to go outside to design or manage their information systems, companies regard writing the traditional RFP (request for proposal) as the next step. They believe that a carefully honed document will enable them to compare contractor bids and select the best. As too many managers believe, "Now you are comparing apples to apples."

Viewing contractor selection from the limited perspective of their response to an RFP can be a major mistake, however. RFPs tend to be long wish lists (compiled from various user groups), with overly detailed hardware, software, and network specifications. Systems performance parameters are also included. These documents are usually not critiqued by would-be contractors (for being overly ambitious or complex, too hardware intensive, or overconfigured). After all, what sensible sales rep wants to put down a prospective client's requirements? (To rephrase the old chestnut, "Any color is fine; the car doesn't have to be black.") Eventually, this document will lead to the structuring of a formal contract, with many or all of its imperfections now ingrained, and penalties attached for non-compliance.

A foreign government developed an RFP for an extraordinarily large, complex information system that would service almost all the public services in that country. One or two of the potential bidders recognized that the resulting system, even if it could be built successfully, would be enormously costly and take years to develop. One thing was certain: by the time it was finished (years hence), the hardware and software platforms that had been so carefully defined would most certainly be outmoded. They would also cost far more and perform less well then the future software and hardware solutions the system would compete with. One contractor actually did seek to warn the negotiators for that country and even sought to propose more modest increments. They were told to bid in strict compliance with the RFP if they wanted to be considered.

Interestingly, all the bidders gave prices that were almost double what the consultants who were brought in to develop the RFP had told the senior public officials to expect. The end result: no company got the contract. The "everything-but-the-kitchen-sink" proposal fell under its own weight. As a result, numerous smaller (more doable) information technology projects that could have made a great impact on this country's economic well being were not undertaken.

Many experienced systems integrators believe that clients unknowingly overstate their requirements and needlessly increase costs and systems complexity. One highly experienced systems integrator believes that four-fifths of the system-generated reports "required" by initial RFPs are unnecessary.

RFPs Often Assume Critical Unknowns Are Known. As typically employed, the RFP constrains potential vendors to bidding on a project fixed in its dimensions and specifications. In many cases (most, in fact, in our experience), it forecloses all the ideas, counsel, and criticism that experienced vendors can provide. It is a waste of the wonderful opportunity this early stage should provide to obtain high-quality, often modest cost, consulting.

Except for minor system enhancements, RFPs often are for a distinctive new system; something that doesn't exist and has never existed. Bidders will be pricing something that has never been done. (This partially explains why there is such a high frequency of failure in these projects.) And the "apples-to-apples" forced comparison is often more myth than reality. Usually, potential vendors will present very different solutions and approaches to the fixed requirements; consequently, cost comparisons among vendors are likely to be "apples to oranges"! For example, a systems integrator can include so-called vaporware (new untried software) in their bid. An unsophisticated client may not be aware of the additional cost, performance, and completion risks this introduces. (This is one of the issues that caused Bank B's outsourcing to be so expensive compared to Bank A in the case study in Chapter 10.)

> (Line manager in Bank B): The RFP specified costly network requirements. These networks would also impact development time frames and maintenance. One contractor had created technology that could reduce the network's complexity, but since all bids had to be in strict compliance with the RFP, that potential saving was never considered by the bank's IT people.

Interestingly, some of the most reputable contractors view RFPs as barriers to a fruitful relationship and a few will not work for what they call an "RFP client." RFPs can introduce rigidities that inhibit successful (i.e., cost saving) performance-enhancing solutions.

Hidden Costs

The most often underestimated cost is the very substantial resources needed to maintain day-to-day coordination and to keep any outsourced function "in the loop." Contractors also frequently underestimate the time needed for their team to interact with the client and learn the business. Most price the project without adequate provision for client input and frequent interaction and exchange of information. Another frequently underestimated cost is that involved in managing the changes that must ensue if the new system is to realize the benefits sought. This is the hard work of reengineering and reconceiving how the organization will work (and change the way it makes decisions) utilizing the new system.

These costs are difficult to quantify and thus never estimated or included in the budget. They generally show up when the system is completed and put into "production." Then those who do the work discover the unforeseen flaws. Neglected end-user needs may be unmet or undermined. End users who have not participated in the system may be unprepared for the changes expected or, worse, reject or try to undermine them.

If neglected, the organization pays a much higher cost later to "sell" the system, retrain staff, and make appropriate changes in policies and procedures, as well as the system, to make it work in a real-life application, if it is to succeed at all. To avoid these pitfalls, any outsourcing strategy must first take these costs into consideration before deciding whether or what to outsource.

Seeking Information Before Bids

Experienced companies have learned a better way. They use an RFI (request for information) as an invitation for interested contractors to come forward, contribute their ideas, and engage in an extended series of mutual explorations. The benefits of this approach have convinced more and more companies that this is the best method for initiating a process for thinking through *the* problem and soliciting potential technically sound solutions.

Instead of seeking to design a level-field competitive bidding war, executives should be initiating a *dialogue* with experienced and interested potential outsource contractors. Astute managers know that the willingness of potential contractors to provide extraordinarily helpful counsel and feedback can be used to their advantage. The ideal is to get these contractors to really understand the business issues of the client and then describe both how they would approach these issues and their technology solution. Good outsourcers know they must invest time in learning some of the customer's business and needs. The customer's assessment of their own situation may be quite inadequate. A sign of a poor contractor is detecting the belief they know the answer before getting any in-depth knowledge. Many fear that probing will be interpreted as incompetence.

The RFI, which casts a broad net in the marketplace, can also uncover potential contractors (motivated, experienced, and competent) who would not have been included in the company's distribution list for their RFP. One of the most important factors to assess is the skill of people who will be working on the project (including your own internal business and IT managers). How able are they to educate, communicate, inspire, and work creatively together in this exploratory stage? Assembling the right team is, in fact, more critical to success than defining what is to be done. So be sure key, high-quality line managers and staff are involved right from the beginning—so they will be learning and assessing at the same time.

A Technique for Structuring the Dialogue

The client needs to control the process by which these preliminary explorations take place. The last thing a customer should want is to have contractors dominate with canned "dog and pony" shows featuring star performers who the client is unlikely to ever see again. It is also easy to be fooled by fancy (and costly) multicolored chart, graph- and illustration-filled proposals. Instead, the client should take the lead in a balanced give-and-take with prospective candidates. Clients may even ask a vendor, "What questions should we be raising with you?"

Some very astute managers responsible for outsourcing give a "technical oral." Each vendor is given a day during which key client participants can closely question them on their proposed "solution" and the value of their proposal. Ideally, the client has been able to insist that the presenters will include contractor personnel who would be involved in the project plan. The client should expect that there will be a minimum of jargon; concepts should be explained as much as possible in nontechnical language. (Professionals who really understand their craft can provide lucid explanations and descriptions in layperson's terms; the less well trained fall back to parroting jargon.)

If an interactive relationship has been established, a good outsourcer will be candid about many of the key trade-offs such as extra functionality versus performance speed, the cost/benefit considerations of a client's wish list, the risks associated with some emerging technologies, and the like.

Legitimate Contractor Anxieties

Contractors have no desire to be exploited by customers seeking free advice, who will "whipsaw" them or carelessly reveal proprietary materials to competitors. An unethical client can turn over to a competitor a potential vendor's costly-to-prepare, conscientiously developed proposal with the promise: "Beat their price and the contract is yours." Obviously, much depends on relationship building and trust, knowing the character and motivation of the people you are working with.

Hiring a Proposal Consultant. At times it may be worthwhile to pay an independent consultant who has earned "high marks" based on their previous work or reputation in the business to work as a advisor to help develop a proposal. That contractor's knowledge and experience may well be invaluable and some thousands of dollars invested here will get paid back many times over in a more sensible project plan.

Site Visits.   Experienced clients also try to visit previous customer sites (where the "short list" contractors have worked). However, they don't want controlled visits. They seek opportunities to speak informally with actual users about what it was like to work with that contractor and their level of satisfaction with the product and its maintainability. Only after these explorations and winnowing will management know enough to write a strong legal document that details the what, when, and by whom of the proposed project.

Making the Contracting Process an Internal Management Review

When handled properly, the contractor selection process itself becomes an invaluable source of information. Management wants to know whether its proposed system solution is the right one. Are there better ways to accomplish the goals? Are there products in the market that already do most of what is wanted? Is the problem management thinks it is solving the real problem?

> A management consultant sent on a mission to an African country to help it construct a larger capacity processing unit discovered that the real problem was not capacity but a bottleneck in the existing technology. Once fixed, there was no need to add capacity; in fact, the problem then became how to increase the supply of the relevant raw material. (Because the consultant had no stake in equipment sales, he saved that country a substantial amount of scarce capital.)

Consultants and contractors often complain privately (too late) that the original solution was misconceived and was actually to blame for the project's ultimate failure or derailment.

> A systems contractor proceeded to design a new travel service interface for a major Internet gateway provider. The contractor

never questioned the requirements or sought to see how the system would integrate with other parts of the client's systems. The contractor did what was asked, and then was surprised to learn later that the solution would never work as defined, given the "back end" the client had in place. (It could not handle the work created by the new system.)

Using Potential Vendors as Consultants. In addition to getting more feedback on the proposed solution, clients and potential contractors should be actively questioning the project's feasibility and searching for alternative approaches, not delimiting them. By adept interviewing of potential outsourcing contractors (those considered "prime" and potential hardware and software sub-contractors), companies learn about alternative technologies and systems approaches. These investigations invariably uncover missed opportunities and unforeseen risks that even the most well-informed executives and system staff (and consultants they may have hired to assist them) will have missed.

The Value of an Exploratory Contracting Stage

A more open-ended, exploratory contracting process can alert executives to hidden problems and prepare them for the complexities and risks that lie ahead. In addition, such a highly interactive approach opens up new opportunities and possibilities. Even more important, it offers the company an indispensable close-up view of potential contractors—when there is this extended give-and-take instead of weighing fixed proposals.

Meeting the Project Manager. Ideally, a client should have the opportunity to meet with the project manager who would oversee the project. There are lots of reasons for this meeting. These technically trained people are likely to be more candid and less prone to exaggeration (time, costs, and benefits) than the sales staff. Their capabilities (experience, candor, wisdom) are one of the most important resources being purchased. And, finally, a great deal of time can be saved in not having to repeat the early stages of acquainting the project manager with the client's business requirements.

Making the Most of the Assessment Process. The contracting stage should thus be an exploratory one in which a client undertakes an in-depth assessment and reassessment of the following:

1. Their own needs, the feasibility and advisability of the proposed solution, and alternatives *in both approach and technology,*

2. The qualifications, approach, and compatibility of various potential vendors.

The assessment and contractor selection process must include line business executives and end users. Never leave the contracting decision entirely in the hands either of internal IS staff or of an outside consultant hired for that purpose.

One of the major bonuses that can be derived from this "learning" approach to contractor selection is that it can give business managers (as well as technical staff) access to the experts with whom they will be working. These managers need to be in a position to evaluate the relevance of fast-changing technologies to their systems or operating goals. Not the least of these is the impact these new systems may have on long-run costs. They should be asking about the future viability and maintainability of the system they are considering outsourcing (versus short-run development and/or operating costs).

Frequently Neglected Criteria in Contractor Selection

All systems contractors and vendors who are equipped to manage information services are not created equal. And most large projects use many different vendors of hardware and software to build the new system. Aware of this, some clients feel the need to hire what contractors call "gatekeepers": consultants who help them evaluate the bidders. But a wise client doesn't shield itself from knowing its vendors—assessing the quality of their product and service as well as their motivation and commitment can mean the difference between success or failure.

How Motivated Are Potential Vendors to Stay the Course

Buying systems development and/or information systems operations requires a good deal of knowledge about the business strategies of the contractor (and—easy to overlook—the business strategies of key subcontractors). It is not enough to have a contractor who has accepted the results of arm's-length negotiation. Most clients have or will discover that they need to outsource to a contractor who is both highly motivated and skilled in making the information system work to the satisfaction of the user.

Thus, the success of the project has to be consistent with (if not integral to) the contractor's strategy—this is the source of motivation to excel. And motivation (beyond simply giving good service for fair pay) is critical because many of these projects are going to be very difficult. Issues will arise in which there is no simple contractual answer. A host of ambiguous, frustrating, and difficult questions such as who is responsible for the problem and how much effort should be devoted to overcoming an impediment (at whose cost) will surface.

- A high proportion of development projects are going to run into substantial unanticipated troubles (from such factors as contractor underestimates of how tough the problems are to changes in client requirements). There will be many temptations to revert to legalistic excuses (e.g., "We just never agreed to do that. You're responsible for the problem, therefore you pay.").

- Some contractors eventually walk away from what seem like insoluble technical problems—sometimes quite rightfully. A bad client can ruin their business.

- Systems design and requirements are inherently ambiguous—even with the most complete outsourcing contract— and many run well over 1000 pages! The contractor must be really motivated to perform in ways that are consistent with the client's business strategies.

- Information system technologies show no sign of becoming more stable. If anything, the rate of technological change is accelerating. Clients are often not able to assess whether their contractor is making the most technologically astute choices and keeping up with the steady stream of advances (and even modifying past choices as new options become available). Thus, the outsourcer's competence and dedication are critical.

- Business users are going to want to make changes in their original conception of what they thought they wanted and even specified. Some of these changes will arise when they actually get the chance to try out parts of a newly designed or contracted-out system. Others arise as markets and products evolve or get transformed and new technological options come into the market.

The traditional textbook methods of project management will fall short of describing what the contractor has to do to successfully cope with these potential sources of derailment. Supplementing these rigorous procedures requires an interdependent set of creative managerial strategies.

Identifying an Outsourcer Who Will Work to Build a Creative Partnership

The following is a short list of desirable contractor attributes:

1. An experienced contractor expects to be learning on the job; they have no "been there, seen and done that" or "plug and play" illusions. No matter how experienced their people are, they know that each project will involve new challenges that should result in some changes in expectations or plans. The client should want to hear that the contractor expects some experimentation, some trial and error

and redirection. The most successful systems development is interactive; it requires continuous on-the-project learning and change and, shockingly, even some failure. Any evidence that the outsourcer is presuming that the contract will play itself out in a simple lockstep structure should be lighting a large warning sign.

2. At the same time, clients understandably look for contractors with relevant previous experience in the same or comparable industry settings. The wishful thinking that past experience says it all must be countered by the contractor's making clear that the *client's specific business context* is critically important.

3. *A wise contractor will want to spend time with the real potential users of the new system and know that will take time and effort.* (Unfortunately, there are clients who expect that good contractors are so experienced that they can be up and ready to begin turning out "product" as soon as the contract ink is dry.)

4. Good contractors are willing to challenge a potential client's assumptions and requirements and help potential clients gain insights they would never have obtained otherwise. They are not so sales oriented (or deferential) that they can't be openly critical of unduly costly and cumbersome client specifications. At the same time, they will be responding to ideas and interests of the client that contradict their own initial assumptions and routines.

5. Good contractors will even help their potential clients develop the questions that an astute client *should be asking competing contractors.*

6. The best contractors allow, even encourage, their potential customers to meet with the key professionals who would be handling the project. (It is especially important to meet with the architect, who is usually very candid and the most knowledgeable person on systems design issues.) They realize that sensible clients want to evaluate the quality of their people, not just the sales staff but those who will actually be managing the work.

7. Many contractors employ an independent *quality assurance* (QA) specialist at critical project junctures. And they provide the client with copies of that assessment as well as access to the outside experts and QA team to thoroughly discuss problems and alternatives. (After all, the customer is paying for it.) Less skilled contractors don't make QA reports available to the client or turn the process into little more than a charade. The best process is one that generates ideas and gives the client and project team the much needed perspective to heed warning signals and make mid-course corrections.

8. The client should expect to receive a balanced, critical education on relevant (and emerging) technologies concerning the proposed project. The better contractors have technically sophisticated staff skilled at communicating with nontechnologists and business managers. They should want to communicate with the real end users in the client organization.

Only armed with this knowledge can key managers become real partners in the project. Indeed, both sides are making big bets (in doing major systems development projects) on the chosen technological direction. The client and the contractor then have to jointly assess how these new technologies will change the way the client conceives of the business and its strategies.

To summarize, clients must seek contractors who will make a major commitment to their project. The evidence is as follows:

1. As high-quality professionals, they will recognize the limitations of their knowledge, the need to assimilate what is distinctive about the client.

2. Their key technical people will be impressive because of their willingness and ability to both communicate and be responsive to user/nontechnical business managers.

Using Contractor Goals

Ideally, the client's specific project should fit the growth and marketing strategy of the contractor. Many times a potential contractor will view a specific customer as a means to gain a toehold in an important new line of business. There also are circumstances in which a customer's systems requirements might become a "solution" that could be resold to others in the same or related industries. Sometimes the motivation is to provide an important proving ground for new technology or a new application for its technology (as the case in Chapter 9 illustrates).

Occasionally, the customer is one department of a large corporation. Effective performance can open other company doors. Some clients get "bargains" or special treatment because they make it clear that they will welcome the contractor's potential clients. They provide them with a "show and tell" tour of their site to demonstrate the excellence of their new system. This kind of reciprocity can be used as leverage by a hard-bargaining customer to get more than their money's worth. Although this advantage certainly can be exploited, it also has some downsides.

The Case of an Outsourcer's Offer That Was Too Good to Refuse

The client was one of the largest and most prestigious firms in its industry. Its current system was running out of capacity and couldn't handle many of their product innovations. It found a major systems integrator who would essentially give the firm what it wanted at almost a 50% discount. This almost free ride was being offered because the integrator expected to resell a version of this system to many others in the same industry.

Wanting to please the customer and hoping to develop an all-purpose customer data processing system, the integrator was never critical of the growing number of bells and whistles that the client demanded. The one finished system would have everything anyone could want in that particular application.

The customer didn't notice that none of the contractor's first team (for this kind of programming) was willing to join the project. (They were put off by the unwillingness of the outsourcer to stand up to and challenge some of the client's expectations.) The system, as implemented, was so encumbered and complex that it frequently went down and could not easily be expanded.

As the firm made heavier demands on the system, it discovered that the system couldn't handle them. In a few years, it was yet again seeking a new system.

The firm was blinded by the great bargain and failed to get a contractor who would design a customized system just for *it*. It ignored the warning sign that the contractor's first team wouldn't work on the project even though it was a large, prestigious contract. It should have sought a contractor who would be a real partner, one who would engage in extended give-and-take. Then the result would have been a more robust and adaptable system—one that would meet its needs over a period of years and provide a stable infrastructure for continuous adaptation and improvement.

The Contract

Statement of Work

The heart of the contract is the statement of work: what will be accomplished and how and by whom. This specifies the resources each of the parties will bring to the project, the numbers and level of personnel that will be assigned, and the number of days they will work. It will make clear the type and quantity of client access and resources that will be contributed. Also included will be the key system tests that will be performed, and, of course, important project milestones.

A balance must exist between what the client brings to the table and what the vendor or outsourcer's decision purview is.

> The Client's Knowledge Base: *what, when, and why*
> The Outsourcer/Vendor's Base: *how, where, and who* [1]

This balance is achieved not by assigning fixed and separate responsibilities and roles for each, but by creating frequent exchanges between technical and business/user teams so that decisions made by one or the other group are informed and improved based on mutual respect and understanding.

There needs to be input from each group about decisions on the other's "turf." While astute clients shouldn't be second-guessing experienced outsourcers by including the *how* in their RFP, they should actively question and seek to understand the pros and cons of the various solutions proposed. Just as important, good contractors should help the client critically evaluate their *what*—not simply accept uncritically whatever requirements or functional specifications are given.

Contract Duration

It is not unusual to read that a major corporation has signed a ten-year, $10-billion outsourcing contract. It is easy to draw the conclusion that long-term agreements are very appealing. They certainly contribute to and symbolize a strong mutual commitment that can foster the building of an excellent partnering relationship. The outsourcer has more reason to invest and even assume short-term losses. There are many downsides, however. Companies undergo radical strategic shifts as well as acquisitions and divestitures that can make contract terms obsolete.

> Sears PLC felt the need to rethink its half-billion-dollar outsourcing agreement when it hired a new CEO who questioned the strategy inherent in the information centralization project launched by his predecessor.[2]

> Oregon's Motor Vehicle Services Department found itself saddled with a new outsourced highly integrated system that impeded the state's new strategy to privatize segments of the work.[3]

Technology also may change radically, making the methods and procedures central to the existing contract needlessly costly. But canceling an existing contract is far from simple and never cheap. More of these issues are detailed in Chapter 7.

Performance Standards

Logically, clients have every reason to expect that the contract will specify clearly what it is they are buying. Further, the client expects that they can use that specificity in their requirements to assure themselves that they will get what they want and what they have paid for. Regrettably (and to the shock of some clients), these presumptions are unduly optimistic.

Flexibility and Creativity. An experienced project manager suggests one specific technique for introducing more flexibility in the traditional contract. Most contracts make some reference to the handling of "change orders." However, it can be useful to make provision for "work orders," which are nonpriced changes that allow work to continue even with ongoing contract disputes regarding change.

New Systems. According to most experienced participants, when a contractor is expected to deliver a unique, new system using relatively new technology, it is unlikely that either party can realistically project the outcome in quantitative terms. Specific goals are, at best, wishes, not the cast-in-stone deliverables that provide a jumping-off place for legal actions. (A not-so-unusual example was described in the *Wall Street Journal* case in Chapter 2 of the legal battles between a division of an Allied Signal and Union Carbide joint venture and their outsourcer, Andersen Consulting.)

A client has to rely on the skills and dedication of the contractor and the quality of the partnership. As trite as it may sound, the final results depend much more on the mutual trust and cooperation exhibited by the two parties than on any written commitments.

Contractors must be willing to devote more resources than they may have intended when intractable problems arise and users must provide a good deal of continuing information about their inner workings and priorities as the project reveals opportunities as well as obstacles.

If the relationship sours and the client seeks to hold the contractor responsible for not meeting agreed-on requirements, there are almost always lots of loopholes—for example, innumerable client changes that occurred during the project can be used to justify those performance deviations.

Defining the Application—Controlling Uncertainty

Different applications will have different levels of uncertainty. Some systems are more modest in scope and involve well-proven technologies. Some represent little divergence from current internal procedures or decision making. The more uncertainty, obviously, the higher the project risk of failure. Thus, one of the main objectives of developing any outsourcing plan is to define the project (including insider responsibilities). An integral part of any plan should be the specification of the responsibilities of insiders and outsiders and the coordination between them. Also included would be the project's phases and implementation strategy in ways that will reduce or control uncertainty. The more uncertainty, the greater the need to determine the best way to break the project down into smaller bits, as you would design an experiment, so that assumptions can be tested and answers used to guide the future course.

Quantitative Measures. The contract should include objectives in terms that a business manager can see and manage. Quantitative, precise standards do have an important place in the contract—they constitute an important part of the *what* that the client defines. However, they must be standards that actual users can see, feel, and consider critically important. (Too often, contract requirements are stated in terms of internal machine performance as defined by vendors; not the work results that management seeks and can independently measure.)

The following, is an example of how one contract clause operationalized a key user's requirements. (The complete case is described in Chapter 10.)

> The client's management team negotiated response time standards for image retrieval based on the volume of letters and inquiries received (plus a growth factor). This and the agreed-on retrieval time from terminal initiation to image viewing were easily measured.

> When these goals weren't reached, the responsible line
> manager was able to use this to negotiate with the vendor.
> They responded by nearly doubling the original hardware con-
> figuration, without cost to the client.

The legal agreement also needs to provide flexibility in its form
and substance. It is critical that the unanticipated reassessments,
learning, and change that occur in successful development projects be encouraged. Building in contractual incentives that focus
on the "what" or end results, in contrast to the "how," allow the
solution to evolve as part of the development process.

Outsourced Operations. Chapter 7 includes excerpts from a contract illustrating how the contract can include incentives that per-
mit client and outsourcer to share the value of improvements or
efficiency gains that the outsourcer develops during the life of the
contract *that directly benefit the client.* Ideally, this increases the
chances that the outsourcer will change its comfortable routines if
the result involves some improvement for the client. Care must be
taken to make sure that such contracts do not include performance
measures that encourage the contractor to do things that look good
on paper but injure other business functions. For example, the outsourcer might get a bonus for beating certain deadlines but might
accomplish this in ways that injure relationships with customers.

Critical Performance Issues Contracts May Ignore

After the client and contractor have agreed on such major performance issues as functionality and response time, a number of other
systems issues deserve concern. These may not be easy to tie down
tightly, but they will affect the client's costs and efficiency over the
years to come.

Once the system goes into production and is turned over, the
insiders responsible for maintaining it learn how well it has been
designed. They quickly discover how many "bugs" or problems will
show themselves, how easy it is to make minor changes (e.g., alter-
ing a product's classification number), add enhancements (e.g., a

manager has conceived of an improvement that facilitates quality control or a hardware vendor has improved their software). Here is where projects put together without adequate testing and reprogramming (debugging), excessive time pressures, deadlines, or overambitious requirements reveal their true costs to a business in time, trouble, and even embarrassing customer dissatisfaction.

Some programs have been written with such complexity and internal interdependency that making any change creates enormous problems. Inserting one new field or calculation may take a hundred reprogramming hours because that field or calculation affects numerous dispersed parts of the software. (This, of course, is one of the daunting problems of trying to adapt programs that blithely ignored the coming of the year 2000.) The change process can be so intimidating to the IT staff (of either the client or the operations outsourcer) that they become reluctant to risk tampering with these convoluted systems.

In contrast, other systems avoid these surprises by adequate testing and preparation, along with frequent interaction between technical and management teams. Prototypes and early experiments help; so does involving the maintenance team earlier in the project development phase so that they are more comfortable and familiar with its design and have input into diagnostic and troubleshooting controls. Chapter 11 contains a good example of the kind of collaborative process that transforms contracts into effective, user-friendly information systems.

Obviously, a "fixed price" contract does not provide the client with the true cost of the system they are buying (as much as the client would like to think that it does). It omits many of the costs of ownership. The costs of maintaining and enhancing the system should be areas of discussion and decision.

What Time Horizons Are Desirable in Contracting?

As the search for the right contractor narrows or the bids on an RFP are being reviewed for a final decision, the time horizon needs consideration. The client seeks an outsource contractor with a long-run commitment to the project and operation. What exactly does long run mean?

- Good people get assigned and the core team doesn't get taken off until major milestones are reached, tested, and revised or fine-tuned. (They are not spirited away just because another project is in trouble or a potential customer needs impressing.)

- Significant emphasis is placed on maintainability, perhaps as much as on the new system's features. (An aspect of maintainability is the guarantee of excellent documentation of the final system. Without this the client is totally dependent on the contractor for the indefinite future.)

- The contractor uses the best hardware available for the job. A key aspect of the "right" hardware—and software— is the vendor's commitment and competency to make continuing enhancements in the future. These are inherently dynamic technologies and being encumbered with a static product ensures gradually decreased competitiveness for the client. (Watch out for consultants and integrator biases based on partnerships and alliances, not competence. If the integrator is also the software developer, make sure that more complete solutions and utilities haven't been eliminated in favor of custom design, as illustrated in the banking case described in Chapter 10.)

Outsourcing Operations

Here clients face some legitimate ambiguities regarding time horizons. They obviously seek a contractor with a long-run, strategic commitment to areas closely related to the client's work. At the same time, the client should be cautious about making such a very long-run commitment. With continued acquisitions, divestitures, and product changes, client needs could change dramatically. Information services technology is changing at an even more extraordinarily rapid rate. Companies have found themselves tied to contractors who are wedded to dated technology (for whatever reason). Cost and services could be improved by changing outsourcers, but that option has been foreclosed by a contract that may run seven to ten years (with significant penalties if it is to be broken). Initially, the client may have received what seemed like a very good deal for that long-run agreement.

Overall, a three- to five-year contract may be the most sensible. A contractor needs that length of time to amortize start-up costs and make a fair profit. And a reasonable period is required to assess compatibility. Jumping from outsourcer to outsourcer, hoping for a magic bullet, is not a rational strategy.

How Binding Are These Contracts?

Contracts can be enormous—3000 to 6000 pages are not that unusual. In theory, every contingency is covered.[4] Most clients assume that a fixed price guarantees a prespecified system at the preset cost. What is ignored is that it really doesn't matter how long the formal agreements are. There are always ambiguities, unforeseen contingencies, and changes. *What matters most is the integrity and capability of the contractor (and the client, of course) and thus the importance of selection.* Every system evolves and changes.

When disputes arise during the life of the contract, and they assuredly will, if the "solution" of the impasse is to turn it over to lawyers, the chances are good that the client will end up the loser. At best, they may get some damages after prolonged litigation. But getting a good system depends on the contractor's completing the task effectively. Even when the contract appears to include objectives that have not been met, most development projects are so filled with changes and modifications of the original intentions (and contract language) that it is difficult to prove that the contractor failed to deliver. With disputes, the goal should be to find a reasonable compromise to *keep the project going and the parties communicating and collaborating.*

The client must remember that it is primarily *buying a relationship, not a commodity.* The system itself is dynamic; it is rarely what was first intended, even assuming that was well understood.

No amount of carefully crafted contract language can build an effective partnership or guarantee a sound interactive working relationship.

Building in Incentives

Clients might want to consider bonuses for systems that perform better than stated in the original specifications.[5] A major airline developed a very astute agreement with a contractor to whom they had outsourced an operation:

> They had experience with contractors who stuck to their routines even though some change would be a major advantage to users. (Limiting change improved contractor profitability, of course.) They now write contracts that rewarded contractors who were flexible and innovative in their operations. And when they, as the client, initiate change, they share their internal savings 50/50 with the contractor.

A similar arrangement exists involving Andersen Consulting and British Petroleum. Under their ten-year outsourcing of some operations, BP has set cost targets and it and Andersen share cost savings equally. (Interestingly, they share overruns the same way!)[6] Ciba Geigy announced in 1996 a contract that gave the contractor a major bonus if Ciba's employees say that they liked the final product.[7]

Selection Is Time Consuming and Well Worth It

Regrettably, companies that have expended a good deal of management time, and perhaps endured some fractious infighting before contract selection begins, are often too eager to get the development of the new system moving. However, the exploration and rethinking that can occur in contractor selection could be one of the most important steps in successful system development. It is well worth extensive time and attention. This is probably the most critical period for any outsourcing decision. It is also the most cost efficient—more can be learned here relatively quickly and inexpensively than at any other stage of systems development.

Experienced potential contractors can be an extraordinarily valuable resource. They can force potential clients to rethink their assumptions as well as their plans and acquaint them with a broad variety of current practice and the best of new technology. Not all contractors are equally willing or able to perform this educational, devil's advocate role. But finding those few is the kind of responsibility that good executives need to undertake.

Some Illusions Concerning Fixed Costs Being Fixed

Understandably, enormous effort goes into the negotiation of cost and performance. Many clients who have not experienced new systems development may then believe they have rid themselves of uncertainty. In most cases this is not true, and not because of outsourcer duplicity. Too many unknowns exist, and most of them will not be recognized at this early stage. The client will discover during development (and often not even until implementation) that innumerable constraints and requirements were buried in the depths of operation. These were not well understood by those who did the contracting and planning for the new system, or perhaps they didn't take the time to exchange and discuss critical trade-offs (probably because they were too high in the management hierarchy).

Only as the process proceeds do users discover that something is unworkable because there is a forgotten constraint in the mainframe system, an absolute auditing requirement, an irreconcilable turf conflict between two functions, or an operational nightmare in the making (a process that looks good on paper but can't be implemented). Procurement strategists have debated the relative value of fixed costs (versus time and materials) contracts for decades. The well-known contractor strategy of cheaply buying into a deal and then adding to profits via the high cost of change orders can work to the client's disadvantage. It is also not to the client's advantage to have the contractor blindsided when legitimate new issues arise relating to the system's design or the technology that will be employed.

There are dozens of ways a contractor can cut corners in doing the actual system development that will work to the detriment of the client over the longer run. (Ignoring the maintainability of the new system and failure to provide good documentation are examples.) Excellence in programming, elegance combined with simplicity, takes more up front time and effort. Both get sacrificed when cutting corners.

Try as one might, the whole risk of a project cannot be transferred to the contractor. The client inevitably bears a good deal. A client must contribute to the design and building of a system that actually meets user needs and has good maintainability. (Many systems developed for presumably sophisticated clients meet neither criterion.) With a reliable contractor and the need for an innovative, unusual system, "time and materials" can be a useful type of pricing. The better contractors say privately that they need to make 20% over that as profit; this is surely not excessive. And, we must remember, there are projects on which the contractor will lose money, particularly those where they knowingly pay an "entry fee" to get into a new market.

Problems do originate on the outsourcer's side. Something they, in good faith, thought they could do turns out to be technically impossible or so complex as to be overwhelming in cost. A new hardware component never gets developed or will be very late. Such problems require more than succumbing to the temptation to blame and seek legal redress. They require a client who will be responsive to alternative programming approaches or adjustments in requirements or priorities.

A new system depended on changes in the prime rate (applicable to variable rate mortgages) being available on-line as soon as they were announced—although the effective date might be days or weeks in the future. The outsourcer discovered belatedly that there were many reasons why the mainframe system could not be changed until one or two days before the effective date of the new prime rate. Initially, that seemed to mean that the contractor could not meet the specifications. However, there was a collaborative relationship. After some analysis of the issue, both parties agreed that a new small application system working off the company's client/server technology would provide this information to borrowers in advance of the mainframe change.

The following chapters provide many examples of what constructive give-and-take actually looks like in the real world of complex systems. It is a very different view from that portrayed by skilled contractor negotiators or IS people who have not had to confront the messiness of operating work. Resolution depends on the construction of a healthy partnership relationship with an outsourcer who will seek creative exchanges, modify plans, and improvise. If problem solving gets hung up on legalistic confrontations over fault or cost, most assuredly the new system will not meet expectations.

Flexibility, creative problem solving, the willingness to "walk that extra mile," congruent goals (between client and contractor) become the important determinants of whether the client gets a system that satisfies or disappoints.

The Key Underpinnings of an Intelligent Client's Contracting Strategy

Most of this chapter and our conclusions deal with the unique problems of contracting for the development of complex new systems or for systems integration. By way of contrast, it is much easier (and more like traditional contracting for services) to establish the terms for writing a simple application system or the maintenance of some equipment. Below are some of the most consequential differences.

- Too many companies conceive of the contracting stage for new complex information systems as the development of a legal document that will be a critical lever for guaranteeing outsourcer performance.

- Not unlike international relations, a contract is no better than the intentions, motivations, and capabilities of the parties. Where these are inconsistent with the agreement or change over time, the agreement's language by itself rarely forces the parties to live up to those terms.

- Inevitably, there will be loopholes and ambiguities that diminish the chances that a strict interpretation of the terms will be made enforceable by legal action.

- Even the biggest and most experienced systems integration vendors will often promise more than they can deliver to get a major contract.

- Every one of these projects is a partnership that depends more on good faith between the parties than on a written contract.

- At the time the contract is written, *neither* party fully understands the client's needs or the technical challenges that will have to be surmounted. These get revealed—and require unforeseen change and adaptation—only during the process of developing the system. Despite the best intentions, almost every contract in this field is based on inadequate or faulty information and premises.

- Those engaged in writing the agreement need to understand this reality and recognize that no amount of carefully crafted verbiage fully secures the client (or the contractor).

Thus, the contracting stage should be conceived:

1. As an opportunity to obtain expert advice on the client's requirements and future system's specifications.

2. As a process to evaluate the relative competency of potential outsourcers.

3. As a means of appraising the congruence between the outsourcer's strategy and commitment and the client's needs.

4. Most important, as an opportunity to assess whether both parties are willing and able to assume the responsibilities of a real partnership: full involvement, mutual trust, and exchange.

Another aspect of partner relationships that is increasingly important to explore is whether the system outsourcer's work is or will be subcontracted. Whether the client recognizes this or not, most outsourcers also use subcontractors who can be critical to project success or failure. Increasingly, work is also being done overseas. What wise clients need to know about "subs" and some of the dangers when their work is being handled overseas are treated in Chapter 6.

Subcontracting Trends and Pitfalls

From a managerial perspective, outsourcing is made more complex and risky when the outsourcer (the prime contractor) outsources to subcontractors or utilizes overseas locations. In everyday language, of course, this is subcontracting.

Information system contractors are increasingly relying on subcontractors. According to a recent survey, 36% of IT outsourcing contracts and 25% of system integration contracts involve subcontractors.[1] Outsourcers subcontract for some of the same reasons that clients turn to outsiders. In some cases, they are seeking highly specialized skills from subcontractors or less costly labor, such as foreign programmers. Using subcontractors can make economic and technical sense for large contractors and their clients. Some subcontractors have carefully honed their expertise in a narrow but important competence.

Outsourcers go overseas for another important reason: significantly lower programming costs in countries like India, Israel, or the Philippines. (Programmers can also be in short supply in the United States.) In many cases, these are captive programming "shops," that is, they are wholly owned by the outsourcer. But their remoteness and culture gaps further exacerbate the risks associated with subcontracting.

The Increased Risks

The increased risks are the obvious ones. More organizations, more "hands" need coordination and integration. There are also more chances that the underlying motivation and goals of all the parties may not be consistent.

What Astute Clients Do

To make the optimum use of subcontractors, clients should:

- Ensure that they are kept informed about the use of sub-contractors. (Some prime contractors fail to make this delegation explicit.)
- Appraise subcontractors and their key personnel with the same diligence used for the prime contractor.
- Insist on having and maintaining direct relationships with the subcontractor.

Astute clients, as the previous chapter concluded, seek to assure themselves that the implicit agendas of their selected outsourcer will motivate that outsourcer to perform with responsiveness, adaptiveness, and excellence. Usually the odds don't favor a similar "vetting" of the subs. Thus, this paradox exists for clients. One of the prime motivations for outsourcing is the desire for one-stop shopping, unambiguous responsibility of the outsourcer for results. But if the client ignores the separate existence of the subcontractor and the need to build a separate relationship with them, it will be making a serious strategic error.

Remembering that the written contract is only a rough outline of what needs to be performed, it should be obvious that the sense of commitment and the resources provided by key subcontractors are of major importance.

Examples of Subcontractor-Based Problems

In the many projects we observed, there were frequent examples of mutual recriminations and classic "buck-passing" between outsourcer and sub(s). It is tempting to shift blame and, given the inherent complexities and ambiguities in systems development, not difficult to find ways in which the other party is at fault for system performance or delays. Thus, without direct contact with the subcontractor, the client may not have a realistic understanding of the threats to the project's successful completion.

There are many cases in which subcontractors have refused to modify their hardware or software to meet the needs of the prime contractor's client. Sure, they have agreed to deliver some part of the system that will meet x, y, and z specifications. But enormous ambiguities still exist and there will almost always be times when the prime has to ask the sub for something that is contractually vague. Then the subcontractor's understanding of the client's needs or their level of commitment (including potential conflicts of interest) can become an issue. And these interests can also shift during a project, especially one with a long duration.

A large systems integrator hired a subcontractor to make special enhancement to the application program used by one of its financial services clients. During a very important large project, another company purchased the subcontractor. The new management had a growth strategy and saw little value in the enhancement for attracting new clients. They wanted to devote their internal resources to totally new software. They provided minimal time and less skilled personnel to this outsourcing project. Major software bugs developed and the project was never satisfactorily completed. No inducements or pressures were effective in getting the subcontractor to take its responsibilities seriously.

Does One Size Fit All?

Often contractors who have designed a system for one client will propose to include it in a package for another. Additional sales will leverage their original software development investment. Beware of this hidden "subcontracting." The savings in time and money you expect (versus designing a system from scratch) can often be deceptive. Software, adapted and modified over a period of years for one client, doesn't often fit the needs of another. And the costs of enhancing prove far more difficult and expensive than anticipated.

The new client will be incurring some substantial risks. Usually this kind of package represents a cobbling together of a number of improvements and changes which will pose two kinds of systems development problems in its new usage:

1. It is likely to be highly inefficient since the parts have been patched together. It probably does not include the kinds of efficiencies that would reflect the most current software techniques and hardware availability.

2. This kind of patchwork system becomes increasingly difficult to customize further. It is very difficult for programmers to work with because so many complexities are embedded in it.

Designing systems that are effective with versatile standards for multiple customer needs is difficult. Many prove to be encumbered by outdated technology and overworked add-ons. Many clients find it is easier and cheaper to build new systems based on the functional knowledge and expertise behind the original systems. Finding the masterminds behind the system can be difficult, however. They can be in the sponsoring client's organization or on the system's contractor team. With large, complex systems, more than one person is often involved and many more could be if the development occurred over a number of years.

If purchasing a previously developed "custom" system, the client should anticipate more time for redesign and even restructuring of the system and make sure the programming team assigned to do the new "customized" system includes those who were intimately familiar with the model system's intricacies and foibles. Otherwise the prime may be incurring extra risks for the client, thinking that they are saving time and money by purchasing a ready-made component.

Irresponsible Subs

Obviously, subcontractors can introduce incompetent personnel. Projects involving subcontractors also run the risk of introducing sources of destructive viruses. A subcontractor on an EDS project for Textron, for example, was alleged to have knowingly disseminated a virus in the client's system.[2] Employees of the prime contractor could also do this, but the dangers are increased as more organizations with varying degrees of personnel control become involved.

Explicit Safeguards

Ideally, the client should choose a prime contractor with the critical systems expertise that is expected to add the most value, rather than having this subcontracted. And certainly the prime contractor should perform a good share of the work and not simply be the coordinator.[3] The client's contract should ensure that work cannot be subcontracted without the client's knowledge and approval. Controlling the number of contractors is a must if you are to avoid the costly interface problems that coordinating with a plethora of subcontractors necessitates.

These issues must be confronted during some of the earliest meetings with a potential outsourcer. Where there is a "red flag," this may well indicate the need to look for another contractor. Clients need to penetrate the wall separating them from their prime contractor's subs. They have to overcome their own desire to ignore this additional level of complexity and the pretense that their big-daddy prime will do it all.

It is also not enough to insist that the outsourcer use only subcontracters selected from a preapproved list. The client must devote time, energy, and resources to assessing the competence and commitment of the key subcontractors *and their key project people*. A potential client for a major system should try to ascertain the motivation of subcontractors, as well as obtain some independent assessment of their capabilities. The subcontractor's interest in the project as well as possible conflicts or alternative demands on their time and energy can be critical to the project's success — no matter how big the contractor.

One small test: Has the subcontractor budgeted adequate time for their project personnel to learn about the client's business requirements? There should be time to meet key client users and technical people whose knowledge will be important in their future work. Subs need to understand the larger system, not just receive specifications for their part of the system as translated by the prime.

Why Bypassing May Be Essential

The more demanding initiatives come after the systems design phase begins. The subcontractor's key people need to become informed about and sensitive to the client's business requirements. It is almost always a serious mistake to assume their induction will be conducted effectively by the prime who may not pass along critical information about the client's requirements and business operations.

Even if it were a realistic option to presume that this is the prime contractor's job, there will still be the need to build some personal relationships with those who will be most responsible for effective performance. There are several reasons for doing this:

- The level of commitment of these professionals can be increased when there is a good personal relationship. Motivation is also enhanced when the client may have future business for the subcontractor or has the potential to become a valuable reference.

- Many trade-offs will be made by programmers in the course of developing a new system. The client wants them to favor the business needs and strategies *not technical convenience* or shortcuts that minimize contractor costs or time investment. Clients who ensure that contractor and subcontractor programmers fully understand the business requirements reduce the risk of suboptimum trade-offs.

- During serious impasses in the development effort there can be extended, even destructive conflicts between the sub and the prime contractor. What gets reported to the client often misstates the reality of the situation. It can be very instructive for client members of the project team to speak directly with their counterparts in the subcontractor organization. At times, insights gathered that way will help the client understand what is really happening and also provide a window into the outsourcer's project team. This kind of reality check gives the client critical knowledge when the contractor discusses the likely effect of project problems on time, cost, or future performance.

Appraising International Outsourcing: A High-Risk Strategy

Clients considering outsourcing arrangements should make sure they know if a service provider uses overseas resources or has intentions of pursuing this strategy in the future.[4] For some clients, the potential for cost savings may be significant enough to make it useful to explore the inclusion of overseas resources. And when programming resources are in short supply, there is an increasing temptation to look overseas. (This trend goes beyond outsourcing. Companies with major software activities have been setting up offshore facilities for some years, particularly in India and Israel — countries with substantial numbers of well-educated workers with lower salary scales than the United States.)

Clearly definable projects requiring relatively routinized programming (e.g., converting certain kinds of reports to a different format) are safer to have done overseas. However, apparent cost saving and availability must be balanced against the enormous geographic, time, and often cultural barriers to frequent, easy interaction and coordination. A great deal of effective new systems development and outsourced operations depends on continuous adjustment between client and contractor and among the various components of a systems development project. Only a small number of these parts can be compartmentalized effectively and "shipped" overseas.

Even subtle cross-cultural differences can create profound communications gaps. For example, it is tempting to presume that in countries where English is the dominant language, say the United Kingdom or Australia, there are few cross-cultural issues. Those who have worked in these countries are always happy to disabuse newcomers of that myth. And the potential barriers multiply among countries with less common traditions.

For some clients, the global nature of their operations may be a significant factor in systems development and ongoing operations. Such activities as foreign exchange trading and international money management are inherently multinational. In such instances, the international competency and experience of a potential vendor are critical, obvious requirements. In general, global resource issues should be explored and clarified in discussions with prospective outsourcers.

Are There Cost Savings?

Early optimism about the ease with which programming specifications could be handed off to the other side of the world and executed by people isolated from the design process has been tempered by the reality of experience. Often cost savings were illusory, given the difficulties of coordination. Even when the need for direct interaction is recognized, it can be difficult to accomplish. The degree to which interactive technology can replace face-to-face communication has been widely overestimated.

There are a host of other problems as well. Outsourcing subcontractors in India, for example, are hesitant to let their staff travel to client countries like the United States. They have learned that they are very likely to lose them to competitors once they are in a place where IT skills are generally in short supply. Thus, an Indian subcontractor may refuse to allow his staff to get additional training or meet with counterparts on a project in another country.

Despite unforeseen pitfalls and early stumbles in attempts to globalize IT development and management, there are now some seasoned veterans and organizations, as well as new technologies, that make global strategies more viable. Nevertheless, multisite projects, particularly international ones, inevitably result in a good deal of long distance travel for key people. This travel, along with early or late hours invested in conference calls, is exhausting. Often there are holdups because managers or staffs have to wait overnight for answers to simple questions. Clients need to recognize that multicultural projects are always high risk. And this must be factored into their outsourcing strategy. In addition to the possibility of traumatic political change, substantial problems can be created by differences in legal systems and even in the importance of law, contracts, property rights, and the like. For example, companies working in some parts of Asia have discovered that copyrights are routinely ignored, as are nondisclosure agreements.

What a Client Should Demand and Understand

Clients should require that the use of overseas resources or subcontractors is disclosed during initial discussions so that they will have an opportunity to assess the risks and benefits of this factor. Clients should not unknowingly enter into arrangements in which a vendor intends to employ overseas resources for even seemingly insignificant aspects of a project or maintenance agreement.

In considering outsourcing with international elements, clients should know that there can be additional costs and specialized resources associated with successfully managing a multicultural project. It would be a high-risk situation to have a contractor who did not have substantial experience with such dispersed projects and had not worked in the country or countries being considered. If international resources are part of an IS outsourcing strategy, the client should carefully consider the extent to which they will be willing to assign personnel to participate in the effort and manage the relations involved. This may include on-site activities and visits or extended assignments overseas.

A Case Study Illustrating the Unanticipated Complexities in Multicultural Systems Development

In the early 1980s, a large systems integrator decided to explore the possibilities of offshore programming for lowering costs, thus making them more competitive. They chose the Philippines for an offshore programming facility. The Philippine educational system specified English as the first language and the country had established advanced training programs in IT.

It was quickly realized that staff would have to travel more than originally anticipated, and that it was important for the general development of the Philippine staff and management that they spend time at headquarters in the United States. Two people in one of the first groups sent to the U.S. headquarters, however, almost immediately left for another job.

After gaining some internal project experience, the integrator sought a client who would be willing to use this approach experimentally. A client with well-established and extensive operations in Japan agreed to have some of its tens of millions of dollars of systems development activity done in the Philippine facilities to gain cost savings. The already complex dynamics of Japanese-American business activities of the early 1980s were made more so by adding the Philippines to the cultural equation. Over the course of this client's projects, the project teams became truly global as members with specialized skills were brought to both Japan and the Philippines from all over the world—at least a dozen different nationalities were represented.

Besides the difficulties of working out the logistics and personnel relations of the projects, several external factors affected the integrator's long-term plans to establish an offshore programming facility in Manila. In an effort to encourage nationalism, the government issued a directive that all education—including higher education—be conducted in Tagalog as the first language rather than English. The long-term prospects for staffing with strong English-speaking skills were jeopardized by this unexpected turn in public policy.

Also, at a critical point in project activities, which were already behind schedule, a political coup occurred, trapping project team members in the office or their hotels and apartments for days and necessitating the evacuation of foreigners on the team as soon as circumstances allowed. At the same time, the outsourcer's local management in Manila increasingly thought of themselves as second-class citizens, exploited by the generally poor economic circumstances of the Philippines. Feelings were exacerbated because the on-site American management team had visibly more resources at their disposal and lived opulently.

Unfortunately, the expatriate manager of the programming facility had almost no management training and little experience, and the same was true of the other managers he brought with him. Yet he was responsible for the start-up of the facility and for tens of millions of dollars in client projects. Needless to say, this also contributed to the sense of injustice and disparity among his Philippine counterparts.

At the project level, the politics of management also played out among staffs who were more often than not caught in the middle. In addition to the language problems and general cultural issues inherent in global teams, the conditions of working in the Philippines were also more of a factor than originally anticipated. Early return rates of team members assigned to work in Manila due to physical and psychological stresses were quite high. This caused more unanticipated disruption to the project activity than expected and eventually took its toll on productivity.

By the time the projects were undertaken, it was realized that client and outsourcer team members would have to go on-site at the programming facility. And team members from the programming facility would need to go on-site at the client's headquarters. The degree to which this was necessary, however, was greater than originally reckoned. Thus, anticipated cost savings were not as extensive as had been planned.

One of the bright spots in this project was that techniques for capitalizing on time-zone differences made for some interesting potential productivity gains. Key developers were working in London, Tokyo, several U.S. cities, and Manila. A plan was devised for handing work from one time zone to another. Code written by a developer in London was tested in the United States, then debugged in Tokyo and Manila by the time the developer in London came back to work the next day! Here distance worked to the benefit of the project.

Another plus was that a large number of expatriates gained international project experience, but this was not an immediate benefit to clients.

International Project Managers

International project management is an emerging specialty among IT professionals. International project managers are a separate and rare breed. They are often multilingual people, with multicultural skills and experiences, who are truly willing to go just about anywhere, anytime, and thrive on the challenges and ambiguity of international contexts. However, these skills and experiences are in severely short supply, and demand is rapidly intensifying.

Thus, it is not unusual for outsourcers and their clients to put inexperienced expatriate managers in positions well beyond their capabilities and experience. Ironically, the expatriate is sent into a situation largely to protect an organization's investment, which may be billions. However, the selection process may be driven by such factors as rewarding someone who asks for the experience or shunting a troublesome manager out of the way.

Given the critical importance of effective communication, key international project managers must communicate with important project groups in their own language. In some cases, clients, sensitive to this aspect, specify a native-language-speaking project manager in their outsourcing contract. Given the general shortage of international project managers, this can lead to vendors installing titular project managers. That, in turn, creates still other problems.

In discussing the language issues of projects, an international project manager pointed out that even if project team members have some language skills to facilitate communication, they are often not extensive enough, at least during the early phases of the project, to communicate effectively. If you don't know enough words in a language, you can sound brusque and totally miss the subtler meanings of words and phrases. It is easy to unintentionally insult someone by misusing their language.

Besides language issues, there may be cultural assumptions made by the parties involved concerning issues like honesty. In one case, a European client appeared to assume that Americans were less honest. It seemed everything the team said or did was treated with suspicion. Even though they would honestly explain the cause of an observed problem, the client would shout, "What is the *real* problem?" This was upsetting for individuals who felt their personal integrity was being doubted.

The Bottom Line

Although the issues that pervade international projects can seem daunting, outsourcers obviously have valid reasons for utililizing internationally dispersed resources. Increasingly, the client's business units are spread around the globe and the need will arise to cross those cultural boundaries. Interestingly, the real return on investing in international activities may be that these situations can highlight issues that relate to all projects, not just international ones.[5]

It is not necessary to cross international boundaries to encounter significant cultural differences. Outsourcing relations inherently involve at least two organizational cultures, and projects often include a myriad of functional and occupational subcultural systems.

Coping Strategies for Cross-Cultural Outsourcing

Geographic dispersion obviously militates against the building of close personal relationships and face-to-face interaction. Contemporary facilitators of communication like e-mail and the Internet and even televised meetings all encourage coordination at a distance. But there is no perfect substitute for the learning and loyalty that develop among people who are in direct contact with one another and evolve mutual commitments.

These handicaps, in turn, are aggravated by cultural differences. The latter provide many potential sources of distrust. Although they may seem imaginary, the effect is the same: hindering cooperation and the willingness to sacrifice for the other person or the larger goal. Clients must protect themselves from the kinds of systems degrading that can result from the absence of a closely knit project. They need to insist that cross-cultural projects be designed so that frequent checks are in place to make sure that the various project components are on the appropriate track.

The objective is to assure project management that miscommunications, misunderstandings, and intergroup conflict are not eroding the integrity of the new system. This gets accomplished through incremental techniques—continuous checks that everyone is on track, everything is current.

Reminders About Subcontractors

It is understandably tempting to assume a simple hierarchy, a single line of authority for any new systems development project. Much more useful and essential is that the client establish some independent knowledge of and contact with the subcontractors.

Poorly motivated or incompetent subs can badly injure a project apart from the motivation of the prime. Clients ought to assure themselves that those selected have the requisite reputations and the ability to perform in a timely fashion. It can be a mistake to rely solely on the prime contractor's judgment or capability to make things right. Instead, the prime contractor should provide information on any subcontractor it is planning to use: financial data, professional qualifications, and previous clients. For example, a subcontractor may have the requisite technical experience but not have a good track record for adapting their skills or proprietary software to the specific needs of the client.

Often subcontractors will need help in understanding the business and its strategies if their contribution is to be most useful. The client is often in the best position to do this. Part of the selection process for subs needs to include their willingness to budget time for this training of their personnel. Key subcontractor personnel can also provide a window on the project and help the client understand more fully the interplay of personal, political, and technical factors. Another viewpoint can often offer greater insight into the project's dynamics.

When the subcontractor is overseas, there are a whole new series of risks that an astute client will seek to assess. Both client and vendor can assume that big cost differences are the only consideration. However, issues of coordination, mutual respect, and timely responsiveness can obliterate many of the apparent efficiencies unless the prime contractor has project managers experienced with and effective in managing cross culturally.

A different kind of challenge is posed when companies outsource continuing operations. How to manage and control these technology management partnerships, using cases drawn from diverse business settings, is described in Chapter 7.

Outsourcing Operations:
The Unanticipated Intricacies

Increasingly, companies are shifting the operation of their existing systems to outside contractors. These outsourcers then manage data processing and telecommunications, client networks, computer maintenance, call centers, and customer service departments.

Many of the most mundane, routine data processing functions are the core of a service-oriented corporate strategy. Corporations have learned belatedly, facing the harsh winds of intense competition, that good service really matters to customers—particularly when other options are easy to come by.[1] The outsourcing of these service functions reemphasizes the importance of tightly integrating insider knowledge and initiative with outsider functions. Where this is ignored, customer service rapidly degrades.

As with the development of new systems, outsourcing ongoing operations should cause client management to confront several issues involving participation of users and the need for continuous monitoring. These functions, after all, are intertwined with almost every aspect of running their businesses. Further, the dynamism of the underlying technologies creates complex and important financial considerations.

Dynamic Interfaces Between Outsourcers and Clients

As we have previously observed, top management often blithely assumes that functions that are candidates for outsourcing are neatly separable from the ongoing business. Not so. Although information services might be considered non-core, they have an intensive, pervasive, and continuous impact on the running of the company. If the operation to be outsourced, for example, needs to be tightly coordinated with internal client functions that are in flux and subject to consequential changes, this should raise some strategic questions.[2]

- Will the outsourcer's requirements impede the user's ability to introduce frequent and even major changes in its products or methods?

- How willing and able is the outsourcer to make changes in its standard operating practices—and how quickly and at what cost?

It is far safer to outsource relatively stable technologies than those that need to be coordinated and updated frequently based on client, production, and marketing changes.

The reality is that contractors can only provide cost effectiveness by maintaining a great deal of standardization. Doing things differently is likely to be much more costly and more difficult to implement than many clients presume. With this in mind, some companies have outsourced the operation of their mainframe systems while retaining the management of their client/server technology. They are continuously changing and adapting client/server technology to meet their needs, while the mainframe applications behind them remain stable.

The Financial Lures of Outsourcing

Not surprisingly, the current wave of cost cutting and profitability enhancement can encourage the outsourcing of information systems related to operations. Whenever these involve technologies with predictable downward sloping cost curves, a contractor can be found who will offer to share *future anticipated cost savings with the client immediately*. Here is how a client's senior staff technologist described a typical "deal":

> We got an offer from a contractor that senior management couldn't resist. They were looking to cut costs and sought out several telecom contractors. The contractors showed graphs of how they saw technology costs declining over the next decade. To somewhat oversimplify, they offered to split the cost savings almost 50-50. So, if costs were expected to decline 60% over the next decade, they would provide our current level of usage at 30% less than it was now costing us—*if* we gave them a ten-year outsourcing contract. As long as our usage remained at current levels, our costs would be fixed at this seemingly attractive "discount." Obviously, if we would agree only to a five-year contract, our immediate savings would be significantly less.

Some contracts also allow the client to seek lower terms if it can identify a competitor who has a more attractive contract.[3]

Some Hidden Costs of Outsourcing Operations

Everyone knows that there really is no free lunch, and the previous example is a good illustration of that homily. Prospective buyers of this tempting "money-in-your-pocket" offer need to factor in the downside to this kind of strategic decision.

Many clients neglect to weigh in the costs they will incur in "managing" the outsource relationships. Liaison, monitoring, and negotiating functions need to be performed, and these can easily add a 5 to 7% increment to the contract's costs.[6]

Contract Flexibility Needed for Operations. Many of these technologies are evolving and experiencing dramatic changes that can't be that easily predicted. Being tied to a given contractor for a decade can turn out to be a costly mistake, especially given the likelihood of new technological breakthroughs. The customer's needs are also going to keep changing. In many industries, acquisitions and divestitures are almost a certainty. And the impact of these changes on the "contract price" have to be continuously renegotiated.

> Remember those fixed-rate 10 year outsourcing deals that stole headlines in the early 1990's. They're history. Flexibility is the new buzzword in outsourcing. . . . Customers must be able to change contracts on the fly to meet business and technology needs.[4]

Many contractors will not have the incentive to keep examining their clients' needs and then propose additional cost-saving or performance enhancements that could reduce their annual billings. In cases where some of the contractor's payment is tied to the cost of the equipment, in fact, there can be an incentive to buy or keep more expensive technology.

It May Not be a Lifetime Contract, but Divorce Is Tough. Even more than design and development contracts, outsourced operations must be conceived as long-run commitments. They are not easily unwound. Various non-outsourced internal functions have been fine-tuned to coordinate with the routines and requirements of a specific outsourcer. And any change is likely to involve an extended period of disruptions in service that is injurious to both efficiency and relationships. (At least some of this may be the product of an uncooperative outsourcer who is losing the contract.)[5]

Often the contracts themselves specify heavy penalties. Very likely, relevant internal IS and IT resources have been dispersed or lost and the user's own know-how has disappeared or become obsolete. This, of course, makes for difficulty in evaluating the additional charges imposed by the contractor for new services that are requested.

Seek Partners, Not Just Vendors

Not only do these need to be enduring relationships, they also have to be real partnerships. Only a very foolish client will simply identify a well-regarded outsourcer with the relevant competence and "go with it." Instead, the customer must evaluate whether the outsourcer is willing to be a "partner," not just a contractor.

The main criteria for partnership are these:

- An outsourcer who doesn't simply "package" its service or accept what clients say they want. It requires an extended exploration of the client's needs, particularly how these operations coordinate with other client functions. The contractor makes it clear that it will be receptive to changes and modifications as users find omissions and new tasks that need to be embedded in the service. Put another way, the contractor is not expecting to be isolated from those who must work with the input or outputs related to the function they are handling.

- A contractor who will continue to explore the cost-saving possibilities inherent in technological advances. It is this expertise that experienced clients expect to buy when they outsource information systems. But an outsourcer must have the incentive to work intensively with the client's internal staff to accomplish this. Only then will they understand the client's operation, products, and customers well enough to suggest where new technology can make a difference.

Many clients hope to receive advice on updating client/server technology, particularly as it interfaces with the outsourcer. A good data processing outsourcer will have personnel who can help clients develop client/server systems that take advantage of host information and, at the same time, create flexibility and adaptability close to client operations.

Keeping the Client at Arm's Length

Often data processing and information systems providers don't really understand their client's operations and needs. They fail to invest the time to engage in broad-based client interactions. As a result, they fail to develop continuous improvements and adjustments and thus the system is never optimized.

Typical is the following case we observed. Here the outsourcer, a large, prestigious consulting firm, was asked to speak with all the division managers (and their staffs) of a diversified consumer products company who had contracted with them to provide all IT and data processing services for the corporation. The intent was to help "educate" the client's management about new systems.

The outside firm spent the entire time making formal, obtuse, and extremely technical presentations. Instead of developing internal competence, the speech discouraged users from extending themselves to learn something about these technologies. In fact, they were intimidated by the complexities. The message they got:

1. These technologies are very difficult for (you) laypersons to understand.

2. There is tremendous competition among technologies and software, so it is difficult to judge what software you should be using in the next few years.

3. You need a firm like ours to make these choices for you; only real experts possess sensible judgments.

Client Failures to Educate Outsourcers

There is another side to outsourcers avoiding their responsibilities to contribute to an educated consumer. The consumer (i.e., the client) may discourage that kind of responsibility. The CEO of an experienced contractor for telecom services we spoke with revealed candidly:

I am dismayed by the number of potential customers we get who just want to turn everything over to us, tomorrow, so to speak. The only way we will work with a client is if they are willing to put together a cross functional team representing all the groups who will have to relate to this service and *who are willing to learn a great deal about what we might do and how we go about doing it.* Then, we have a group of our own, experienced with managing such teams, who will spend many days working out the specifics of what is needed and how it should be provided. You can't get that from a piece of paper or contract terms that a client has written.

Outsourcer–Client Coordination

Some well-regarded contractors make it difficult for their clients to develop needed coordination. An officer of a very large U.S. commercial bank we spoke with describes some of her problems with outsourcers.

We make a good deal of use of contractors on our retail side. I am always amazed at how the larger, more sophisticated contractors don't make it easy for us to coordinate with them. For example, on some of this work, we need a meticulously programmed daily "feed" to our mainframes. The person working for our contractor, who is our designated liaison, never seems to understand the requirements. And, as they seek to find the right person in their organization, our requirements often get bungled. In contrast, in smaller outsourcers you can usually speak directly with their programmers.

We have also had other problems involving short-term outsource contracts. One division was planning to contract some telemarketing and new applicant data entry work. Several contractors, in different locations, had to be used to handle the expected short-term volume spikes. To main-

tain control, the data was supposed to be fed back (trans-
mitted) to a central client-managed system, where it could
be monitored for accuracy before updating the host system. The contract, however, didn't require this interface,
and one of the contractors was preparing to update the
host on-line. This would have undercut our carefully
designed management controls. Because this requirement
hadn't been spelled out, it was very difficult to get them to
"walk that extra mile."

Those involved in drawing up the contracting agreement obviously need to have some intimate knowledge of the coordination
issues. They also need to design the contract so that operational
coordination can continue to evolve and be perfected. Broad, boil-
erplate type clauses and contracts that are fixed in stone have no
place in a world of dynamic technologies and markets.

What level of system downtime can the client afford? Naïve
clients sometimes ignore the downtime issue. In the telecommunications case in Chapter 11, management made it clear that they
could only tolerate two minutes of downtime, max, per day. That
placed very imposing restrictions on the system's design. More
clients probably need to specify their tolerance for downtime as
well as understand the implications for continuity of service in
the contractor's regularly scheduled maintenance and emergency
procedures.

Specifying response time and performance objectives often
involves trade-offs. This is an area where candid communication is
needed between the business client and the IT outsourcer. Specifications that are too high (i.e., restrictive) can undermine or inhibit
necessary maintenance activities, development, and system
changes that a client would want the outsourcer to do.

Excessive Pressures on Outsourcers Hurt Performance. The
business client also needs to understand the impact on system performance of changes in system specification and enhancements.
Trying to do too much too quickly often results in cumbersome
and complex systems, riddled with costly performance and maintenance problems.

The need to continually appraise system performance, both responsiveness and downtime, cannot be overstressed. It is easy to observe the amount of business or customer good will that is sacrificed when computers go down in a department store or the retail division of a bank and no transactions can be processed.

Client/Outsourcer Interdependence Is Usually Understated

The departments that will either input to outsourced operations or use their outputs have developed a large number of procedures for internal coordination. Many are second nature and largely undocumented. When interacting systems or operations are outsourced, these critical links often disappear with the "insiders" who managed them. Even outsourcers and vendors who have had vast experience with conversions have a tendency to avoid researching these details. They prefer to impose their own routines and ways of doing things on the client. By insisting that they need certain routines, they believe they are protecting themselves from pressures to introduce costly modifications. The better vendors, however, have learned to thoroughly examine and understand the client's pre-conversion operation. They've discovered that this is essential in planning for a transition that will facilitate a smooth changeover—one with the least impact on the client's customers and business. And sometimes a change requested by a demanding client can improve the outsourcer's service for many clients.

There is substantial research documenting that the interfaces (between tasks or departments or elements of workflow) are much more complex than management realizes. Even slight "misfits," that is, failures to interlock or coordinate properly, can create enormous costs.[7]

Astute clients select a contractor who already is working with sophisticated users in their industry. They don't assume, however, that other clients will have demanded operating parameters that are exactly like their own. They interview the clients and take the time to tour their operations and talk with people on the job. Even then, there will be a learning curve for the outsourcer. Good outsourcers realize that even similar clients in the same industry have unique requirements that need attention.

Outsourcing an Operation: Airline Travel Packages

The often unanticipated client/outsourcer problems associated with coordination need to be viewed in the workaday detail of an actual company. In the following case, the outsourcer assumed that the client's initial, very general description of what it wanted was adequate. It was not until after taking over the operation, that the outsourcer realized the complexities of the system and the degree of training and experience necessary to be effective. If the client and outsourcer had not maintained communications and coordination, neither the candid acknowledgment of problems nor the working out of solutions would have been possible. The contract would have been a failure.

Best Travel Services

A major airline outsourced the booking of some of its vacation packages to a contractor with a strong reputation in the travel business, Best Travel Services. Senior management, who negotiated the contract, saw this as an easy way to reduce the overload their company was experiencing in their reservations area. The marketing division also saw it as a way to get more attention to this specialized add-on service that they felt was being neglected by their internal operations.

Because of internal conflicts over the handling (and internal cost allocation) of this operation, the move to outsource was made precipitously by the marketing division, with little consultation with Reservations. There was no conception that this was a complicated operation.

When it was being performed in-house, the best and most experienced customer agents were used. They had developed a complex and largely undocumented series of procedures to facilitate bookings. These agents knew the reservation system inside out. They worked outside the training books and procedures, finding their own shortcuts and work-arounds, as many long-standing operations personnel have learned to do. They knew what data was unreliable or mislabeled. Some of the best agents were assigned this new travel package work and had discovered how to adroitly interact with customers while waiting for their sometimes slow mainframe processing.

The marketing managers knew only that they wanted to transfer the business with the least amount of service interruption—and so required Best Travel Service to use the same reservation system that had been jury-rigged to handle this add-on service.

Best assumed that the business was very much like the other travel booking services it had been handling. It had optimized its own system to handle travel packages and reservations, but readily agreed to use the airline's system. It also left the system training entirely up to the client. The client's procedures were also adopted in accordance with its standard training documentation procedures book, not after an actual review of operations.

Once operations were underway, Best realized how unprepared their agents were to handle the new system. It was confusing and complicated, and procedures were unwieldy. Service standards were immediately impacted and customer interaction was clumsy. Best had added a number of new hires to handle the new contract and the results were a disaster. These employees were inexperienced with airline bookings and, of course, unfamiliar with all the tricks of the trade that airline agents had developed.

Best soon realized that their training and procedures were inadequate, and that they needed to get a far greater understanding of the airline's total operation. They then devoted the time to understand the system with its foibles and idiosyncrasies and sent a reengineering team in to see how agents actually used the system. The results: new training and procedures, and much more time spent with new hires to develop the necessary skills for handling these functions. Best bore much of this cost, but the airline also suffered the consequences initially in loss of sales and customer confidence.

Outsourcing an Operation: Customer Call Center

Another case illustrates a different set of coordination issues. Almost every company now subscribes to the critical importance of customer service. In a variety of industries, however, that "service" is increasingly provided by "professional" call center service providers who employ sophisticated computer-driven information systems, usually working off the client's host mainframe.

The following is a finely detailed description of the complex dynamics of the client/vendor relationship in an outsourced call center operation. The amount of "fine grain" give-and-take may come as a surprise to most senior managers who consider this kind of outsourcing routine: "Ship it off to an outsourcer and we're done; it's their headache now." In this example, however, we see the opposite—a client management alert to what they must do to make their outsourcing effective for their needs.

Alton Magazines

Alton Magazines is a company that has struggled with the complexity of outsourcing its subscription management and servicing functions. It has learned that managing the outsourcer relationship is not simply a matter of cost control. Service operations are anything but stable or "passive." Alton found that for an outsourcer to manage a key component of their operations effectively, an enormous amount of coordination was needed both within their own organization and with the outsourcer's.

Alton publishes a number of magazines. One of the largest outsourcers in their industry handles their fulfillment function and information system (mailing, subscription list management, and customer inquiries at a large call center). The service provider has expanded rapidly, through acquisitions and new business. In recent years, the publisher had grown somewhat concerned that it may not be receiving good service, but had difficulty documenting this unease.

Alton brought in a consultant to do an independent review of its outsourced operations as well as evaluate its internal procedures and standards for measuring its effectiveness in:

- Delivering high-quality service to their customers (subscribers)
- Retaining and building customer relationships
- Gathering customer intelligence—for policy and marketing decision making

The consultant, working with Alton senior management, focused on the outsourcer's quality assurance and operating standards. In general, the relationship was a strong one and demonstrated many positive practices. Because these both were growing organizations with diverse objectives, however, there was a need to constantly manage the relationship to maintain an effective partnership.

Gradually, Alton, working with their consultant, introduced a number of changes in the relationship. Problems were identified and resolved that would improve service. But, more important, new systems and incentives were developed for monitoring performance so that service improvements could continue to be made.

The operational issues the review surfaced may appear excessively detailed. However, a client's willingness and ability to be concerned with the precise specifics of how their work is being handled are what make the difference between effective and ineffective outsourcing of operations.

Staffing and commitment. Ensuring that the staff assigned by the outsourcer to Alton were not merely knowledgeable but strongly committed to the magazines had been one of Alton's chief concerns. With that in mind, they had ensured that their contract stipulated that (a certain number of) staff be "dedicated" to Alton. (This requirement was later changed to a goal that would have 85% of calls answered by dedicated staff, making both outsourcer and client accountable for watching volumes and optimizing staffing levels with their fluctuations.)

Feedback and innovation. Alton realized the usefulness of agent feedback on customer concerns and issues both in monitoring the performance of operations handled by the outsourcer and their own editorial, advertising, and marketing policies.

Alton had established, on site, a company liaison who regularly reviewed mailing and subscription service fulfillment activities. In addition, Alton periodically sent marketing representatives to visit the outsourcer's call center. They supplied free subscriptions to their magazines to service agents. And Alton marketing representatives met regularly with them to discuss customer and any other concerns. Alton understood how important this was in developing an agent's identification and support of Alton, as well as with its products.

One of the outgrowths of this regular dialogue with service center staff had been the development of a number of "exception" handling procedures. These included procedures for waiving fees, extending the subscription period, and rectifying any billing errors on the spot. Alton also received a number of reports from the outsourcer detailing call volumes by product and call handled (and abandoned) rates. Additional reports provided detailed information on customer renewals and response to different direct mail campaigns.

Alton's management of their outsourcing activities was, in fact, much more hands-on and sophisticated than most. They were pro-active in promoting their products to representatives and took the feedback they received about marketing and subscription renewal strategies seriously. Based on this feedback, Alton actually started a number of new programs that encouraged renewals.

Insights into vendor's system problems. This direct contact and regular interaction with service staff also made Alton aware of limitations in the vendor's mainframe system. It found that it was difficult (if not impossible) for the vendor's service reps to effectively bridge different systems to cross-sell products—one of their customer retention goals. With sophisticated questions and staff, Alton established a strong, trusting relationship with the vendor, who respected them and wanted to maintain their substantial business.

For some time, the vendor had been promising to implement client/server technology using intelligent work stations that would help overcome these mainframe problems, but other system priorities were in contention for resources. The vendor, however, was actively courting new business and its attention was focused on growing the business.

Often companies mistakenly think by outsourcing systems and technologies, they will no longer have to deal with these kinds of resource contention issues. In reality, many outsourcer systems development queue's are dedicated solely to new business, or consolidation of new business acquisitions. They have little time to revamp their core systems. Quite the opposite— they often make core systems more vulnerable to downtime and system performance problems with quick fixes designed to cope with the needs of numerous new customers.

Risking competitive advantage. One of Alton's vendor's ambitions was to develop a new revenue source, an information system that would tap the growing demand of their clients for more data on their customers. They hoped to utilize much of the knowledge they had acquired working with Alton and other publishers, who had developed sophisticated list management systems.

Alton had done most of its customer profiling for marketing and renewal analysis in-house, using file extracts from the outsourcer's host system. The outsourcer now realized that developing this capability itself would represent a lucrative new marketing opportunity. Many of the ideas it was now pursuing, in fact, were conceived in its relationship with Alton. (Here was a clear case of the risk customers sometimes take in outsourcing partnerships. Partners can often take advantage of the specialized knowledge they gain in these relationships. In this instance, a lucrative new business niche was established by siphoning off the hard-won knowledge of the client.)

Monitoring a vendor's internal employee performance goals. To improve service times and call answer rates, on which the vendor was judged, agents were given service handling goals (calls were expected to be answered within an average number of seconds). Unfortunately, this is a frequent performance evaluation measure. While it is useful to look at frequency distributions of average service time, and review and more closely monitor agents whose numbers depart radically from the expected range, setting specific call duration goals can cause some very counterproductive behavior. One obvious one involves shortcutting the customer; another is increasing the number of callbacks because too little time is devoted to solving a problem.

Instead, Alton wanted agents to be evaluated based on how well they were providing service to customers. Initially, the outsourcer objected; their costs had been predicated on a certain level of agent "productivity." Alton proposed a program of assessing call handling based on the degree of point-of-contact resolution. It also set new goals with the outsourcer that rewarded them for finding ways to improve this resolution. As procedures (and some of Alton's own policies) were changed, customer problems and requests could be handled completely in one call. The result—less need for repeat calls, which translated into fewer calls and lower servicing costs or greater service capacity.

Alton agreed to share the productivity savings (or capacity increase) with the outsourcer. (The outsourcer's revenue had previously been tied to an expected level of call volume—this change removed an impediment in the overall service improvement goals.) Customer calls were now not just listened to, but recorded and evaluated for ways to improve customer retention, operational quality, and efficiency.

A dedicated team. Alton had wisely insisted on having a dedicated service group to handle their calls within the outsourcer's organization. (They had also invested time and money in training this group.) The call statistics they received, however, didn't allow them to evaluate how many of their calls were actually taken by the dedicated staff. A new report was added, which disclosed that the majority of their calls, during peak periods, were being off-loaded to a larger pool of staff who handled many different publishing and magazine clients. Consequently, customers were getting staff less familiar with Alton's magazines and business and untrained to handle many of the exception processes Alton had authorized.

Alton also discovered that the vendor was using many of its more experienced agents in this back-up group. The vendor preferred to use these more experienced agents here to handle many different clients, with unique systems characteristics, policies, and procedures. The dedicated group was thus being regularly depleted of its most skilled and experienced staff, leaving more trainees handling calls on the "front lines." This diluted the effort Alton had put into training and developing agent commitment and interest in their products and services.

Alton worked with its outside consultant and outsourcer to determine the optimum staffing configuration that would ensure that the majority of calls would be handled by their dedicated group. The total numbers were not very different from the original estimate, but new schedules had to be worked out with their outsourcer to guarantee that more dedicated staff were there at peak calling times.

The new service commitments changed the goal from a fixed number of dedicated agents to one that allowed for staffing flexibility with the goal of maintaining that calls be answered by the dedicated team 85% of the time. Alton also became an active partner in helping to forecast volumes, alerting and preparing the vendor well in advance of special marketing initiatives.

The new service commitments then became part of a regular monthly review Alton held with its outsourcer. The outsourcer and Alton used these sessions to become more attuned to the impact of their actions on the service quality and operational effectiveness (and profitability) of each other.

Learning How to Make Continuous Improvements

In outsourcing situations, the larger goals of retaining the client's customers or recognizing and reporting when a policy or process is causing customer dissatisfaction unfortunately are often ignored. The outsourcer usually is content to leave routines intact (and undisturbed). And the client can easily lose touch after the hand-off. There are no reports or data (especially those defined at the time contracts are drawn up) adequate or sufficient to ensure that ongoing operations coordination is effective.

To maintain high quality and effectiveness, both partners must be willing to work collaboratively. As we have seen, nearly all improvements require complementary adjustments. This is difficult enough when everyone involved works for the same entity. The challenge is even greater when they are separated organizationally and (usually) physically.

Managing change and trying to influence a client are difficult and create more work and even uncertainty for the outsourcer. So the client must keep this dialogue going and give the outsourcer incentives to seek improvements and new opportunities. In Alton's case, this closer partnership resulted in many changes that involved system and operational adaptations on the part of their outsourcer:

1. New reports and call evaluations got Alton and its outsourcer to do some reengineering of its systems and operations. One improvement: a long-standing customer complaint was resolved when operations were reengineered so that new subscribers did not get billed before they received their first issue.

2. The joint planning of a new graphical user interface (GUI) used agent feedback to help define cross-system customer information and cross-sell or offer replacement aids.

3. More attention was given to customer retention (subscription renewals), including new statistics for reporting agents' success with various retention offers. These provided valuable marketing feedback on these offers and other practices.

4. New incentives were also established with the contractor that rewarded them for making or suggesting changes that improved service quality or increased retention.

What Is So Meritorious About Alton Management?

Alton was fortunate in its choice of outsourcer. Although this company was very successful and had a fine reputation, it wanted to keep improving its own information systems and felt it had something to learn from a sophisticated user like Alton. The relationship had a good deal of embedded trust; neither side felt the other was trying to "pull a fast one." They also realized that the goals of quality service, customer retention, and the capturing of customer intelligence are all profoundly impacted by the quality of feedback companies get and use from the regular contacts with customers that occur in the normal course of business.

They knew that one of their toughest challenges was to get close enough to their customers to obtain that feedback. And they were willing to take the initiative to make sure that outsourcing a customer-intensive function, like their call center, did not leave them more remote from their customers.

Persisting Challenges in Monitoring Outsourcers

As Alton's experience surely demonstrates, an outsourced operation requires substantial monitoring. Companies outsourcing operations engage in self-deception when they count as savings the elimination of their IT staffs. Line managers, coordinating with outsourced operations, need to continuously keep in touch with and monitor performance. And they will need a core of talented IT and functional specialists to both monitor and work with the outsourcer to ensure that the changing and evolving needs of users and customers (of the client) continue to be translated into systems reality.

Hard-dollar costs are affected by the absence of adequate internal staff. Information system technology is so dynamic and the product and service market so broad and volatile that a buyer can't be content with "purchasing" a good name.

What Is Effectiveness?

Outsourcer effectiveness goes way beyond the usual comparisons of direct costs. Too often, evaluations of the advantages of outsourcing are limited to comparing how much is being charged and how many jobs can be cut. Assessing the relative advantages of outsourcing should force management to think more broadly about the function being outsourced and its relation to other parts of the organization. In the Alton case, for example, call centers do much more than handle complaints. They have inputs to marketing and they can save customers.

The issue is not just one of outsourcer effectiveness; it is also one of client effectiveness. Outsourcing clients need to take into consideration the cost, talent, and time needed of in-house staff to monitor, measure, and maintain effective communications with operations it no longer directly performs.

Over time there are bound to be client changes that will require cost or systems changes on the part of the outsourcer. The *worst* way to handle most of these will be to presume that the full answer has to be in the original contract. A typical contract might specify that the outsourcer will handle *x* number of transactions in a given time period. For example, the contractor developing a system for handling all the imaging associated with a major credit-card operation agreed that their system could handle a certain volume of inquiries, called "chargebacks" in the context of many other transactions.[8] In fact, because chargebacks involve repeated contacts over time with bank customers, merchants, and merchant banks, they utilize a great deal of computer capacity. Only after the system was in operation could this aspect be fully comprehended.

Asserting the contract is not the most constructive way of dealing with this kind of issue. In this case, the client and contractor explored ways of modifying the client's internal chargeback workflow that would reduce the load. In turn, the contractor agreed to provide more capacity than had originally been planned. Of course, this kind of mutual exchange, in contrast to legalisms, is what partnerships are all about.

Critical Dimensions of Outsourcing Operation

The following are reasonable assumptions that every client should include in their decision calculations.

1. Very experienced outsourcers will have developed routines that will not be totally compatible with existing client sys-

tems. This means that there will be transition problems as internal systems are reconfigured and personnel retrained. Often these are hard to identify until work begins, so they can come as a surprise.

To overcome these difficulties, you want an outsourcer who will take the time to get to know your operations and processes and is prepared to adapt its own systems and procedures. Avoid firms that want only to fit your business into their routines. They will not have developed the skills needed to coordinate with your business needs, much less continue to adapt to new technological advances as they are made.

Vendors with these traits and skills for working in partnership with your business's needs also have learned to involve (and respect) lower level managers, who know the intimate details of existing workflows and business requirements.

2. Most operations have more complex dimensions than are usually appreciated. How the "details" are handled may be more relevant to the real costs of outsourcing than any contract price. *Thus, a system is only as good as the user/ system interface—never better.*

A good deal of managerial attention must be paid to the precise specifications (and definitions) of information (data): how various operations and users within the organization (and their customers) will collect, use, and analyze information, what actions and turnaround times are expected, and so on. Asking a potential outsourcer about whether they handle particular activities using certain procedures may well produce a "yes" when the real answer is "no." This is not because they are seeking to be deceptive but because many terms are ambiguous. To be sure that both sides are talking about the same phenomenon, a good deal of in-depth exploration is required. The goal is not merely to assess the degree of congruency or contradiction between the outsourcer's and client's routines and expectations, but to evaluate the outsourcer's resourcefulness and skill in understanding and responding to your needs.

3. Be careful that the "team" that courts your business is not overselling (and overcommitting). There can be a big gap between promises and services that get delivered. And most contract penalty clauses will not compensate for the degradation in service or loss of customer confidence that may ensue. Nor will there be a rebate for time lost in the race for advantage in the marketplace.

In most cases, the client can anticipate having battles with the contractor over whether changes are *enhancements* or *new development work*. The former are usually included in the overall price, while the customer is expected to pay in addition for the latter. A legalistic contractor can always find ambiguities here.

4. The client also needs to keep in mind the possibility that some competitive advantages will be lost. The outsourcer may well share with other clients any operations improvements or innovations developed by or with that client. There is also a growing trend for outsourcers to start new businesses selling a variety of information and technology services based on their growing technological know-how in certain niche businesses. At some point, these non-outsourcing products or services may become competitive with their client's products.

The greatest assurance that the outsourcer's activities will fit well with the client's need—and with the right price—is the active involvement of middle managers. They must be encouraged not only to participate in negotiations but to undertake information system initiatives that complement the larger systems that may be outsourced.

The next several chapters explore three unusually successful outsourcing relationships. These real-life examples depict some of the tough problems and many of the effective managerial interventions and solutions discussed in this book. Chapter 8 is an overview of these several "how-to-do-it right" case examples.

Three Superb Examples of High-Performance Partnerships

Managers responsible for three highly successful systems development projects have described the success factors associated with their challenging information systems in very different corporate settings. These new systems are in major industries undergoing rapid technological change and using substantial information systems outsourcing.

1. *Financial services* (customer service imaging system)

2. *Telecommunications* (solving operating problems)

3. *Retailing* (developing a data warehouse)

These cases provide an unusually candid and intimate "insider" view of the issues confronting executives seeking to improve their use of information systems. The reader can thus view tough problems in the dynamic, everyday context of executives and systems professionals coping astutely with a changing array of challenges. Their descriptions of what was done, why, and how, offer guidelines for others who seek to avoid the typical pitfalls and traps encountered by many of the participants we encountered in our studies.

125

Different Industries and Technologies— Important Similarities

The three cases provide a very different view of outsourcing from that held by most client executives and many information service providers. Success is not primarily a function of the right plan, getting a good contract, and the best price. The process is far more complex than the usual, very simplistic, linear decision sequence:

1. Decide what is wanted and develop a sound RFP.
2. Put it up for bid.
3. Review bids carefully and select the best offer.
4. After development, implement the new system.

An Up-Close View of Partnering

In two cases (retailing and telecommunications) the "what do we want" was the product of a creative partnership between client and contractor. They each were able to bring to the table separate bodies of knowledge. Obviously, the client had an in-depth knowledge of the user's world and business objectives. But the contractor had complementary knowledge—the capabilities and limitations of the technology.

Both understood the need to spend a great deal of time and effort in this process of understanding client needs and the relationship of those needs to a new technology. And there was a continuing exchange. At times, the client modified its requirements in the light of technology costs or potential; other times, the integrator/systems developer shifted away from its preconceptions about the appropriate technical solution.

The financial services case, by way of contrast, illustrates how much clients can do for themselves *if* they have two key resources:

1. A line manager/user willing to assume responsibility (and risk) and unafraid of new technology.

2. Hardware and/or software vendors able to work directly with users to facilitate the adoption of their technology.

Substantial Client Involvement

All three cases are excellent examples of the major themes of this study. Clients can never afford to be passive when outsourcing the development of new systems. Their active role must extend throughout the entire cycle, from planning through development and implementation. Only with the intimate involvement of their end user can the client obtain full value for the capital costs.

The Right Outsourcer. There are enormous differences among outsourcers. When the client can find one whose goals are highly compatible with the intended project, they can obtain extraordinary assistance both in shaping their expectations and customizing a superb system.

Stress on Incrementalism. The development process itself has to be an incremental one. Neither contractor nor client should anticipate that carefully conceived plans are ever truly complete or realistic road maps that show the way to a winning conclusion. Many unanticipated obstacles will require changes, fine-tuning, or workarounds of various kinds. Users will find inadvertent omissions; more important, they should be able to see new requirements as they learn more about the developing technology.

There is a premium on continuous learning, thinking on your feet, fluidity, adaptability—a managerial perspective usually totally absent from traditional organizations and from traditional precepts of project management.

Truly successful new applications of systems often look quite different from their original conception after full implementation. Again, this reflects the dynamic interaction among users, vendors, and the valuable learning that goes on as the system develops.

Knowing Effective Partnering When You See It

Almost every buyer and seller (of information technology services) speaks blithely of partnering with each other. In most instances that we have observed or that have been documented, there is less there than meets the eye. However, these three cases illustrate robust partnering. The vendor/contractor/integrator recognizes, from the outset, that a great deal of patient (and costly) effort must go into understanding the real user's needs. (These users usually aren't those who sign the contract.) It is the beginning of the project that is the most critical (and frustrating). In both the telecommunications and retailing examples, great effort went into designing a prototype that would both test and refine the joint effort to understand user requirements. In the financial services case, much of the exploration took place after the user selected a relatively standard imaging and document management systems package and sought to design a workflow system to facilitate the division's unique requirements.

Both contractor and client continuously and mutually readjust their expectations of what is required, learning from each other in the process of working through the original conception and jointly working on the development and implementation. Both expect that there will be trial and error—on-the-job learning—and thus neither outsourcer nor client have rigid, "cast-in-concrete" demands. The project is fluid and incremental.

These cases are an unusual resource for outsourcers and clients because key participants provide in their own words an almost real-time account of what actions made the difference.

The next chapter is a superb example of how one of America's best known specialty retailers was able to implement a totally new data warehouse after earlier failures.

A Nationwide Retailer Discovers the Power of Data Warehousing

We have chosen this outsourcing example for several reasons. Data warehousing is an important thrust in the information technology field. It is also a technology fraught with high cost failures that yield little tangible results. But here is a retailer and vendor who developed a highly creative, productive partnership that produced dramatic benefits.

The term "data warehousing" refers to the use of new technologies (usually parallel processing, scaleable systems) to store enormous quantities of data that can be easily interrogated and analyzed using relational data bases. These systems are also often referred to as decision-support systems, when their analytic power is used to help make or support marketing, product distribution, inventory, and purchasing decisions. Their potential for "mining" data, another term commonly applied to describe their ability to go through massive amounts of detailed information about customers and transactions, has captured the attention of business decision makers and technologists alike.

Fancies (not its real name) is a highly successful nationwide retailer (with more than 500 stores) and the billion-dollar division of a very large corporation in the upscale fashion clothing field. With the increasing visibility of data warehouses, Fancies' management wanted to at least explore this rapidly growing technology.

They hoped to provide their merchandise buyers (who have relied substantially on past experience and good judgment) with a powerful new tool that would shape both purchasing and distribution decisions.

Initial Failure to Develop a Data Warehouse

Fancies' first attempt at implementing a data warehousing system to store and retrieve a wide range of information about customers, suppliers, and buying and usage patterns proved a failure. They engaged a highly respected integrator and outsourced the technology decisions and development of the data warehouse. The project was funded from the top with an ambitious enterprise-wide plan and driven by the outsourcing contractor, who sought little participation from buyers and company insiders. This project was abandoned some $10 to $30 million later, riddled with technical problems and scuttled by the indifferent buyers who saw no tangible value in this high-tech extravaganza.

Lessons were learned. The company's prior foray opened management's eyes to some of the headaches and performance problems of building these huge data bases. It was no longer willing to jump in without strong proof that the technology would work to solve real problems. Fancies' managers also knew that given the corporation's concerns with earnings and further investments in technology, no new top management commitments to information technology would be made unless they paid for themselves—quickly.

Contracting Strategy: A Unique Request for a Proposal

Fancies realized it had substantial leverage to obtain a very favorable contract. After all, it was a highly prestigious retailer—a successful project would be "money in the bank" for a systems contractor. Presumably, lots of other clients would then be attracted if the systems contractor demonstrated product leadership in its work with Fancies.

Seeking a Contractor Willing to Invest Heavily Up Front

Fancies developed an RFP for a first stage. The company would contribute a small budget, substantially less than $100,000, toward this preliminary feasibility study. The winning contractor would be expected to invest substantially more in people and hardware to develop the feasibility prototype in collaboration with Fancies' managers. The demonstration would have to prove that a particular technical platform could cope with a huge data base, interact with core legacy transaction processing systems, and be valuable to line executives in making buying decisions.

The contractor was thus expected to have substantially more at risk than the client. But if the study provided significant business justification, then a major investment in a data warehousing system would be made and the contractor would automatically get the business. More business could also be forthcoming from other equally large divisions of the parent corporation. That was the hook. And it worked.

Fancies' presumptions proved quite accurate. Several contractors made bids and were eager to fund the pilot as a means of penetrating the retail market. They knew they would be collaborating with a highly successful retailer known for being savvy in its management methods. Fancies was thus able to "pay" for this first-stage project largely by its high visibility and prestige in its industry, not by cash.

Selecting the Right Partner. Fancies' information systems people expected that the bids would be for a PC- based system to do the proof of concept for a contractor proposed system. And that was what they got by way of bids. However, one prospective contractor argued that a PC-based model could not possibly be a realistic simulation of the fully functioning data warehouse. The project manager (PM) of the winning bidder described his reasoning:

> There are very real dangers of relying on a PC-based proof-of-concept to demonstrate the real capabilities of a full-blown system that would have to manage inquiries that need to relate to tens, even hundreds of millions of records. In addition, it would have to test the links of any

future system to the "legacy" (existing mainframe data storage and retrieval) system for data inputs and decision outputs as well as provide high availability, timely analysis for rapid decision making.

That argument proved decisive when bolstered by the vendor's offer to supply some substantial hardware free of charge for several months. The PM selected by the chosen vendor also had an extensive background of experience in retailing as well as in systems. After getting the assignment, he selected a small technical staff to work with a counterpart group of experienced manager/buyers from the client's organization.

This stage generated great enthusiasm because the vendor was working closely with the buyers who would be directly affected. Any approach would thus be the product of their joint explorations, not simply the expertise of the PM and his staff. Together they sought to answer some very straightforward questions concerning current purchasing, inventory, and stocking decisions.

- Are there ways to improve profitability at both the store and individual product levels?

- What are the limitations of current information resources for making the kinds of decisions that should determine these micro profitability levels?

- What are the advantages of tracking sales and on-hand history for every one of their hundreds of stores using a powerful data warehouse?

A Strategic Approach to Project Scoping

Instead of spending many months defining all the ways data could be looked at and all the kinds of data that could be stored and retrieved in a powerful data warehouse, they developed an action approach. The PM had the team identify the products and data inquiries that would be the best test of the potential of this new technology and its impact on increasing profitability. The intention was to target their efforts and learn what they could about a single product line and the details of each transaction: store, style, size, color, and so on. (In fact, this single product proxy for all their merchandise eventually became a huge data base of its own.)

The PM discovered in these early meetings that Fancies currently managed each store's inventory on the basis of its conception of *an average store* in its chain. Thus, for popular items, some stores could be experiencing stockouts, while others had surplus inventory and might even have to use markdowns to move the surplus.

At this stage Fancies' senior management were quite skeptical. They doubted that this data warehouse approach could provide consequential additional profitability. The conventional wisdom was that the average in-stock level was close to 95%, with almost no shortages even for popular items. They assumed there would not be much leverage in improving inventory management from a large (costly) data warehouse.

The simulation was designed to test this assumption and explore whether day-to-day management decision making could be improved by seeing whether Fancies could achieve better distribution with the same or even less inventory.

Design Specifics

The product line selected represented one of Fancies' highest margin lines, where even a little improvement would have an immediate bottom line impact. The actual data warehouse prototype design included twenty-five styles of product in each of the chain's stores. Key data on sales and on-hand numbers by store were extracted from the everyday sales transactions of these items. Each store's product performance measured percentage in-stock (by size, style, etc.) and gross margin return on inventory. Overall, the prototype required 100 million rows of data and was intended to have merchandise managers (the buyers) use this data to make actual order and inventory decisions. This trial system would interface in real time with Fancies' host system.

Early Favorable Results

As the team explored the data for this product, they learned that inventory decisions based on the old "average store" inventory method were, in reality, highly inefficient. Out-of-stock levels of popular items were much higher than management had believed.

Very positive results occurred when management began actually using this prototype data warehouse to make inventory decisions. The PM was elated to report that the system was paying for itself within the first *ninety days* of the trial by effecting real (not simulated) decisions. As the PM recalled,

> Fancies was able to increase sales by 40% on one item in an important region by customizing the inventory model for individual store sales with the new data warehouse. Other stores with slower sales on that item "financed" the increased inventory in the faster selling stores by reducing their own inventory levels. Everyone on the team was able to recognize the obvious good will benefits of being in-stock with the same assortment in every store—*without adding investment in inventory*. In fact, we were able to lower overall inventory levels by creating higher sales volumes. And, of course, profits were also bolstered by decreased markdowns.

Gradual Expansion of the Project

The underlying project strategy followed by the PM was *incremental*. Working closely with the managers who were the real users, the PM facilitated their mutual exploration of the potential of data warehousing for additional products. And these explorations were self-funded—by the savings being created by each previous test product.

As the usefulness of the data warehousing prototype became apparent, the business team for the project increased to twenty-five users. They now began to explore the full range of management decision making that might be enhanced with a data warehouse. Among the subjects covered: improving pricing, varying regional assortments, alternating approaches to markdowns, increasing turnover (making way for additional fashion seasons), and evaluating a wide range of promotion strategies (e.g., at what point in the fashion season do special promotions provide the greatest stimulus value?).

The users came to realize that data warehousing could also be used to promote and support local initiatives, which could have a profound effect on a management decision-making structure which heretofore had been highly centralized. Local initiative could be efficiently and unambiguously tested, assessed in a specific market, and, where successful, expanded to other stores and markets (and contracted where unsuccessful). Local stores sensitive to their customer needs could thus take initiative with central management comfortable that results could be quickly assessed, countered, or fine-tuned.

Getting Feedback in Real Time

The technical project team also learned from their experience. They encountered puzzling delays in response time and called in their hardware engineering group to discuss ways to improve the speed and accessibility of data. By testing the actual system architecture with massive quantities of real data, the technical team was able to identify weaknesses in system performance. These were brought to the attention of the hardware vendor's engineers, who found the bottleneck in the technical platform and removed it with just a few modest changes in the operating system. The speed and responsiveness that resulted represented a real gain, not just to this application but to the vendor's future effectiveness and success with data warehousing applications.

Often this kind of hardware engineering feedback, much less change, is nearly impossible. But here the client was working directly with the hardware vendor (who was also the contractor). This company was committed to making the system work well. Such responsiveness of the committed vendor meant that systems problems were not ignored or blamed on "slow learners" or obstructionists in the user community.

Another application design flaw was also uncovered and resolved. Originally every item in every store would have its sales record updated every day. So a typical item might sell in a store once every ten days. The original software design would produce the same record every day for nine days (of sales and inventory for that item). With the engineering change, only one record would be created on average every ten days (when a sale occurred). But the software was able to create the other nine records from data in memory if they were required for some computation. This relatively minor program economy saved an enormous quantity of data storage without compromising the need for business metrics that require passive inventory data.

Had there not been this close relationship with the hardware vendor, an outsourcing contractor might have wasted thousands of dollars reprogramming a clumsy work-around to cope with the performance problem that had been identified by users (slow response time). More hardware probably would have had to be purchased to process what was essentially passive data.

Incrementally Scaling Up

This data warehousing project has continued to grow, step by step, as its users gain greater familiarity with the technology and its potential. It is important to keep in mind that the prototype was not a model or a simulation, but a scaled-down version of a real data warehouse. This meant that the user/participants in the project could actually obtain real-time, actual data decision support and could thereby assess the actual power of their new data warehouse. As comfort levels grew, so did the range of applications explored.

What Can Be Learned from Fancies

This very successful case highlights the enormous potential of high user involvement in incremental systems development. Instead of starting with *the* plan, Fancies' management decided to engage in an extended exploration of the specific profitability enhancement that could be provided by a customized data warehouse. They sought and found a development contractor willing to assume a significant share of the initial cost to acquire the opportunity to win a major contract if the "proof of concept" proved successful.

The hardware and systems vendor, noted for its scaleable, high-volume technology, was anxious to gain a foothold in the retail business and eager to prove its superiority in this burgeoning arena of data warehousing. Unlike most prototype projects, designed in a PC environment to give users a "feel" of whether the approach is sound, this one was designed as a fully operational system on a major computer system. Thus, it didn't just simulate; management could actually use the prototype as a real-time decision support tool since it could handle enormous quantities of real data.

This learn-while-you work approach proved very fruitful for the following reasons.

1. A system was developed that was almost perfectly attuned to the needs of client/users. Even minor clumsiness in the system was not tolerated as it would have been in so many other comparable developments. In those, improvised work-arounds and lowered expectations take the place of a system's excellence.

2. Users actually experienced what it was like to have a data warehouse to query and stimulate decision making. The interplay of line managers with the technology became a highly creative experience for managers. It was a sharp contrast to their prior venture. Instead of a full-scale new system in which critical decisions as to what it will do and how are made by outsiders, the users had the stimulus of real exploration and the power to accept or reject it—there were no phony participation games.

3. As we have noted, the actual system gradually evolved as a result of user experience, not from before-the-fact grand plans.

4. The contractor was willing to keep learning and changing in response to needs that revealed themselves during development. In turn, it was able to make the hardware product and the system an even more effective tool for data warehousing.

A Hard Won Victory for the Vendor

Almost a year and half after the experimental period began, Fancies signed a significant contract with the vendor to supply a full-scale system. In the larger corporation, eight levels of management had to sign off on this new contract! As the project manager described the approval process,

> At the end we (the vendor) didn't have to sell anything. The client's users sold the organization and the CEO. We started at the bottom of the organization and created win/win scenarios. Previous vendors had sold the corporation's top management very large projects. These got approved and developed with little input from users. Often they represented major technical leaps into the future (that then fell far short of the mark in execution). The actual users, left out of the whole outsourcing process, had little patience for the predictable imperfections and delays. And they allowed these massive impositions on their routines to fail. Call it passive aggressiveness or indifference, users had no real role in the development process.

It was the direct user generated business input and involvement, more than any other factor, that made this initiative so highly successful.

Credit cards obviously require powerful information systems. Chapter 10 is an unusual example of how a resourceful line manager can use a well-chosen outsourcer to build inside-the-company technical competence. Many executives may be surprised to see how much a business manager willing to learn about new technology can accomplish.

Bringing Imaging Technology to Credit-Card Operations

Being able to observe two almost identical systems development projects in similar companies that employed totally opposite management approaches is most unusual. Even more extraordinary are the differences in the bottom-line results of these new systems. This unplanned "natural experiment" confirms many of the recommendations we have been making that grow out of our larger study of outsourced systems development projects.

Both new systems were designed to improve the efficiency and effectiveness of back-office operations for the credit-card divisions of two large commercial banks. Both banks had millions of card holders and were introducing imaging technology to cope with the tens of thousands of documents flowing through their operations each month.

The Experiment — Two Banks

This chapter follows the step-by-step progression of two application development projects. Companies continuously add new software to better manage their unique business requirements. The rich detail of this case description vividly illustrates the incremental methods by which involved line managers and end users can reconceive their work as they gain an intimate understanding of the potential of automation. It also demonstrates the kind of vendor and outsourcer relationship that stimulates and supports learning and adaptation of both technology and operations as applications are developed. When combined with an innovative vendor/outsourcer, these strategies and tactics produce remarkable results.

The description and analysis that follow are provided by the project's sponsor who occupied a key line position in Bank A's credit-card division. This same manager was also in a position to observe a comparably sized institution's (Bank B) management decisions to develop a similar system application. Their management strategies were totally different—as were the bottom-line results.

Bank A

In the first case, a middle-level line operations manager spear-headed a largely do-it-yourself development effort. This initiative relied heavily on the day-to-day working experience of insiders and the advice and assistance of a major vendor of imaging technology.

A's successful management strategy was line-manager driven. A vendor of an integrated family of technology products for imaging and document management, the FileNet Corporation, provided many of the services of an outsourcer, although there were no special costs associated with their consulting services. (Imaging technology converts paper records into digital form so that they can be computer stored, retrieved, and manipulated.) The line manager and FileNet developed a real partnership, far more collaborative than the usual relationship between buyer and seller.

Bank A obtained state-of-the-market (not state-of-the-art) software and hardware technology. Bank A's manager/sponsor committed to a 25% return on investment in imaging technology that began with an investment of $750,000 in hardware (and associated software and development tools), a thirty-five workstation network, including optical disk library, printers, and scanner. As applications of the system expanded, the network grew to eighty workstations for a total hardware investment of $1.5 million supporting all aspects of their credit-card correspondence handling operation, new account acquisitions, and fraud detection. Applications were designed in-house, using just two programmers at the start.

Bank B

The costs to Bank B were variously estimated but exceeded $5 million in consulting fees alone. Cost comparisons are hard to make because the system scope and managerial approach, as well as functional and performance setbacks, added significantly to the costs as well as to the cost-saving benefits of the developed system.

Management Contrasts

Bank B's impetus for change came from an executive responsible for credit-card operations and an associate in the central systems group who was responsible for "emerging technologies." Credit cards were thought to be good candidates for imaging technology. B had outsourced its host credit-card processing system (accounting and statement sending) and its operations were highly manual, with virtually no use of personal computers. The project was conceived of as a major enterprise-wide initiative that would update all aspects of credit-card operations.

Having little internal experience with these systems, B hired a major systems consulting firm to design, select, and then develop the best system. It believed this firm would be able to transform the organization's operations and bring it into the twenty-first century.

The dramatic difference in results came not from the decision to outsource development, but from the way the applications were designed and managed by each organization. The collaboration between technologist and operational management along with the methods Bank A used to promote the participation of end users proved to be the most important difference. These resulted in Bank A's gaining the sought after productivity and quality benefits from their imaging technology investments. Bank B's management learned the hard lesson—that automation and the profound changes in process and operations that need to take place to gain their benefit cannot be "imposed" from without, but must be developed and supported from within the organization.

The comparison shows that the effectiveness and the success of this system development effort depended on:

- The degree of involvement of the end user.
- The commitment to continuous improvement (versus a "one-shot" innovation).
- The use of off-the-shelf, well-developed technology versus seeking to push for state-of-the-art technology.

Bank A's business managers directed the design and programming of the new system and through their experimentation with different ways of organizing workflows made major reengineering changes, reflecting a very different approach to handling documents and paper flows. They also became more self-sufficient in innovating new functions and capabilities of their system applications.

Bank A's Automation Strategy

Bank A's new applications development project was begun because the operations manager was troubled by the impact of cumbersome paper processing capabilities on both costs and customer service. (This also provided Bank A with its first exposure to the value of imaging technology.)

The following narrative is Bank A's operations manager's description of problems and how she undertook the selection of a vendor for new hardware and software.

Many of the tasks performed for customers took too long and were too labor intensive. It was increasingly difficult to control the large number of documents and records needed as our credit-card portfolio grew with major acquisitions. We managed two large service organizations and were looking for ways to improve the speed, accuracy, and personal responsiveness to customer inquiries. In-house mainframe system resources tended to support marketing initiatives and shortchange back-office operations. Meanwhile, service was slipping as the bank's operations grew, and it was not unusual for customers to wait thirty days for a response.

Credit-card research operations (required when a card holder disputes a charge for example) were complex and entailed financial risk for the bank. The rules for adjudicating cardholder disputes over purchases made with Visa and MasterCard were time consuming and required excellent control over documents that moved back and forth between banks. To resolve a problem that involved another bank's merchant often took months, and hundreds of thousands of dollars were at stake. Where we failed to act in a timely fashion we could lose so-called chargeback rights, an expensive penalty.

The Manager's Description of the System Search and Selection Process

Our first thought was not imaging—which in early 1984 seemed too expensive and not a solution to our document management problems. Instead, the manager of the customer service research operations and I were exploring microfiche and CAR (computer automated retrieval) systems. This technology was proven and relatively inexpensive. I was close to making a decision to go in this direction when a systems manager responsible for exploring new technology suggested that we look at what imaging could do. He introduced us to one of the leading vendors, FileNet. The costs did appear high—but the capabilities went far beyond electronic filing.

FileNet was eager to introduce us to others who had applied the technology, some in contexts very similar to ours. We made several trips and had lengthy visits to observe the system in production environments. The ability and willingness to show us actual sites where their equipment was being used in settings comparable to the functions we were managing were critical factors in our selection. There were not many imaging vendors at the time who could demonstrate their capabilities this way. We wanted to watch the technology in action in a high-volume production operation, *not* in vendor demonstrations.

We also wanted to interview our counterparts in user organizations to see what they had learned. I was amazed at how forthcoming other users, even competitors, were. Line managers and their technical staff who had lived through these projects shared "do's and don'ts" that eventually saved us enormous amounts of time and money. We gained another object lesson from these site visits: the importance of a technology that allowed for adding "home-grown" applications and the ease in performing maintenance work. These factors proved to be as, if not more, important than price and features. The systems "workflow" system was easy to learn and adapt. The hands-on nature of this system, we later realized, made all the difference in continuing to enhance and further its utility.

Gradually, we began to get a fuller appreciation of how important it was to obtain imaging hardware that had built-in workflow capabilities. We were seeking a total system, not simply a storage and retrieval capability. That is, we wanted to automate the sending of documents from one workstation to another as well as capturing data from our mainframe and the using it to create user-friendly screens and documents. Rules and procedures were embedded and helped employees resolve customer inquiries. We also wanted our research staff to be able to generate a broad variety of letters to customers, merchants, and other banks. The "form" letters would be in memory, ready to be customized by staff, the system automatically transfered names and amounts from the host screens to the form letter.

FileNet was unique, at the time, in having software that was totally integrated with its hardware. Together these provided total system capability. These built-in "proprietary" functions, later faulted for not being an "open system," actually cut down the complexity of the system and the number of vendors and interdependencies we had to deal with. Competitive pressures have now forced FileNet and others to become more "open." But the well-touted benefits of interconnectability and open systems have lagged well behind their "plug and play" promise, leaving technical and operational managers in a constant battle of determining responsibility among a host of interacting vendors and software providers.

FileNet also had an active users group. They received significant feedback here, finding what their most experienced customers wanted and deemed important. Such feedback was behind their workflow software that encouraged and facilitated a do-it-yourself approach.

Conceptualizing the New System

Our early explorations of what imaging technology could do led us to a completely new vision of its application. Instead of just looking at the problem as one of file management, we saw that this kind of system could transform the way work was done. It could change the way we interacted with our host system, automate the use of screen data to avoid mistakes in calculation, adjustments, and letters, and eliminate data entry and proof and control functions as we had known them.

We realized that we needed to look at the entire research and correspondence function, not just access to data and records and the control of incoming documents. The manual processes we used were fraught with risks and cost and we began to see how this new technology could help us overcome them.

Most correspondence dealt with customer complaints about charges to their account or credits for returned or deficient merchandise or services. Bank letters communicated with customers to request more information or sales slips from the customer or to explain procedures or policies affecting the claim. The correspondence function also communicated with the merchant's bank, requesting information or refunds (if the claim seemed valid). The customer's letter and the sales slip formed the relevant evidence supporting the claim. Research staff had to select from over fifty Visa and MasterCard codes for identifying the reason for the disputed charge, each with different supporting requirements. An error made in selecting the reason code, in insufficiently or incorrectly documenting the claim, or failing to meet rigid turnaround times between banks could all lead to bank losses as well as customer complaints.

These steps could also require repeat letters when customers failed to respond adequately or the vendor's bank failed to respond, lost the initial correspondence, or denied the claim. It was not unusual for some item to get misplaced or for misinterpretations to occur as a result of sloppy handling and poor handwriting. Each communication with customer and the bank representing the merchant generated paper that a data entry clerk would then read and enter into the system—a labor-intensive operation full of potential error.

Keeping track of all of these steps, being able to access specific letters quickly, updating the related files as new information flowed in, and composing accurate, attractive letters to all the parties constituted a huge, "backbreaking" coordination task. Frequent errors occurred, along with a great deal of wasted motion.

Costs were high, not just in terms of the workforce, but because of the nature of the credit-card business. Being late with a letter to a merchant's bank or failing to have all the data could result in losses. At any one time, hundreds of thousands of dollars of charges were in dispute; thus, the risk of operating losses was significant.

Proving the System

FileNet's imaging system's workflow capability had opened our eyes to an entirely different way of managing this awkward, error-prone operation, but how to start? System investments were not made lightly in this company, but we were convinced that the technology would produce demonstrable savings in efficiency.

The success of other companies using this technology and the savings they had achieved in their operations spurred our efforts. In addition to the expected file maintenance savings, we saw that we could perform adjustments on the system and transmit files to update the host, thus eliminating a very time-consuming and costly manual adjustment process (including data entry, proof and control, and reject/reentry). The writing of form letters, word processing, and editing could also be eliminated—with specifically designed customer responses, automatic completion, and letter generation. Using the system to calculate adjustments for finance charges would vastly reduce errors and thus rework.

Getting Funding

We were not sure a capital investment of $750,000 in this as yet relatively new technology and hardware would be approved, even when we were willing to commit to a 25% savings in productivity improvements. (We had already planned to use resources within our own budget to fund programming and maintenance of the new system.)

The request for funds to purchase went before the bank's Research and Development fund board. The board was enthusiastic, but—ironically enough, given our confidence in its cost justification—recommended that the division fund it within its own resources. Fortunately, the division head responsible for this part of the organization had confidence and was willing to risk the experiment.

Getting Started

It was still a bootstrap operation. We started with two programmers. We had gotten the equipment purchase itself approved by showing a very fast payback. (Eventually, we were able to demonstrate that we saved the almost million-dollar capital cost in less than two years!) At first, the head of the credit-card systems group openly opposed our vision for the technology; he called it "naïve."

Within my own department, I found several employees interested in learning to do programming. They were trained by FileNet to design "workflow systems" using the software application development tools that the vendor had developed (and that were included with the hardware purchase). Most important, these employees knew the intimate details of our operations.

We were thus able to use both experienced programmers and develop into programmers experienced research staff who showed the aptitude and interest. Blending technical and operational know-how in the programming team was one of the most effective means of gaining firsthand understanding of the technology and its capabilities and the difficult task of reconceiving how work would get done. For the more complex technical problems and issues, we called on FileNet's technical reps, who provided consultation both on design and ideas for improving overall efficiency and organization of the workflow and tasks.

Staff, who were doing the work, were extensively involved in the actual details of the design. We had regular meetings with the people who handled certain kinds of customer complaints or questions about accounts. These focused on the specifics of screen design and work processes. End users decided where and how data was to be displayed, how much per screen, and all the little things that they felt would make their work both easier and more accurate. They were reengineering their own jobs.

Handling Operating Problems; Partnering with the Vendor

As we began using the new system, we had two kinds of problems. One was capacity; the other involved the system design. It was at this point, after the system was rolled out and running, that I was able to appreciate our vendor's "partnering" orientation toward its systems customers.

I had negotiated a contract with the vendor that guaranteed that the equipment they sold to us would be able to handle our peak loads. Their technical people had spent some time with us "sizing" the requirements before we agreed on the size of the order. When we encountered delays due to overload, I contacted the vendor. Initially, there were negotiations over whether volumes had grown beyond our original specifications; I had specified that the system would be able to handle three times the volume (expecting that we would eventually integrate all service center operations) and was able to show that the combined volumes, in fact, were not greater than this estimate.

The vendor worked on a number of solutions, including conducting a rigorous review of the efficiency of our programs. It recommended some changes here as well as in some of our maintenance activities—and added more diagnostic software to measure performance improvements. Performance did improve, but not enough. Although the contract had called for equipment to be added if performance did not meet criteria, the vendor could have fought or delayed this action. But it instead agreed to loan us additional equipment to handle the overload. (The hardware would be returned when and if the vendor was able to make improvements in their technology and software that made the additional equipment unnecessary.) There was no need to involve our legal department (although they had reviewed and signed off on the original contract). The vendor was committed to resolving the problem.

There were many more examples of implementation fine-tuning that the vendor provided to improve system capacity and throughput:

- Earlier the vendor helped us employ an enhancement it had developed at other user sites that also served to stretch the system's capacity. It enabled us to cluster workstations so that the system would treat them as a single unit.

- FileNet also showed us how response time could be speeded by preselecting (into ready memory) documents that we were most likely to be working with on a specific day.

- Another operational problem that was slowing us down revolved around the need for microfiche files of data no longer residing (and accessible) on the mainframe. Often a customer problem required checking these older records and it was very time consuming to do it off-line. This kind of need and similar needs expressed by other system users apparently had propelled the vendor to develop some innovative technology that would store the microfiche on optical disk and convert it to an electronic image so it could be retrieved and viewed. We took advantage of this to store and get quick on-line access to statement data going back two years. This speeded up customer response times as well as eliminated costly microfilm retrieval functions.

- We had offered the vendor work space at our site for its regional technical representative and to store replacement parts and software. Our in-residence field engineer provided an enormous amount of continuing advice and assistance. And, of course, we got replacement and upgrade components faster.

Continuous Learning—Refining the System

As we used the system and tripled its volume by integrating remote site operations, we discovered that our original design had compartmentalized functions too much, resulting in some of the "buck-passing" defects of the manual process flow. Employees were losing site of the whole and supervisors became frustrated. We all agreed that the best way of resolving the problem was to create small teams who were completely responsible for handling all aspects of resolution. Inquiries would be assigned to one team who would follow through with the potentially multiple interactions with banks and customers until the problem was completely resolved. Different team members might be involved at various stages, but they worked together as a team to take responsibility for solving the problem and meeting the time constraints. Each team got reports that tracked new inquiries and what was outstanding at every stage of resolution. Team leaders were thus able to see the whole at a level of detail that had only previously been possible for the department head. With this broader responsibility and control of the work, the teams quickly learned from feedback from banks and customers how to adapt work strategies in ways that radically reduced rework and inefficiency.

These gains, while outside the system itself, would not have been possible without the control (and feedback) that the new imaging system made possible. The new system design facilitated control over work cycles, which, in turn, facilitated continuous learning and adaptation on the part of teams doing the work. Productivity gains became continuous, and were not simply realized as an immediate and direct benefit of the system implementation. Insight into how the system could best be used to improve results thus came from hard-won experience.

Unfortunately, for many organizations, the benefits of this kind of learning are rarely permitted. System development funds and personnel resources are used to support new initiatives. Postdevelopment systems improvements are treated as low priority maintenance enhancements. Here programming resources were dedicated to the business unit, and became part of a continuous learning process. Furthermore, we were working with a system that could be readily changed due to its programming ease and adaptability. Many more changes (although somewhat less dramatic) were made to increase efficiency, provide management information, and add functionality as we gained more experience and confidence. The value of these modest reconfigurations only become clear when a real user sees the system in actual operation.

Quantitative Results: The Bottom Line

When the system was fully operational, we reduced the time required to respond to customers by 75%; thirty days dropped to two or three. (Customers were delighted with the improvement in service.) And our organization was able to absorb a large, newly acquired portfolio (twice as big as our own) with *half the staff*— Almost a 100% improvement in productivity.

Continuous improvement and maintenance of the system were provided by three programmers who had been trained while they worked with the technology. This not only eliminated a good deal of costs, but, more important, provided the means by which improvements conceived by the manager and her staff could be implemented, almost overnight, and continually perfected.

And employee morale soared. Many of the sources of job frustration had been eliminated by the new technology, and employees responded with relish to their involvement in job design.

The following is a summary of what managers can learn from Bank A's experience:

- With increasing ease of programming, an energetic line management can accomplish a good deal with modest cost systems development with vendors who are organized (in this case through a well-trained sales department) to aide users in walking through the required steps.

- At least some new information technologies can be very empowering for line managers willing and given the opportunity to develop and learn to use them. There is no need to know programming or become a computer scientist. As generalists, motivated managers can learn the basics that enable them to make informed choices and guide the development and implementation process. Since they know best their business needs and priorities, this is an almost ideal scenario. They are also best at making the cost/performance/time trade-off.

- A true partnership can develop between the vendor and the customer. The Bank A sponsoring manager sought to be fully involved in systems implementation: learning, designing, and experimenting with alternative ways of using the new system. The vendor had as a primary objective the satisfaction of the customer: aiding them to achieve a working system that would meet their operating objectives. FileNet did not focus on who was at fault as the system became operational and problems emerged. Quite the contrary, they sought solutions—just the kind of attitude a customer hopes to find in a vendor (and should seek when choosing one).

- Employees were involved with the changes. In doing some of the fine-tuning of jobs for themselves, they became more committed to the new system and made significant contributions to improving its effectiveness. (One of the inherent benefits of these technologies is the ease with which employees can make contributions—for example, to determining what information gets displayed, when, and how.)

- The customer was constantly learning, at the nexus of everyday work problems and the new technology. The system was treated as a "work in progress" and thus problems were not disasters but opportunities to experiment with change, often in collaboration with the vendor.

Bank B

Bank B had been relatively backward in introducing computer technology and their senior management wanted to essentially "leap frog" the bank into the twenty-first century. They had minimal confidence in the technology capabilities of their line managers. Thus, total responsibility for a new system to automate credit-card functions was given to a systems integrator. This outsourcer had carte blanche to choose the new technology and design the system.

Bank B spent millions of dollars seeking to create (overnight) a grander system. Bank A spent 10% of that for a system that had 90% of the functionality and substantially better performance.

The contractor did not present the relative advantages and disadvantages of various technological solutions. It chose state-of-the-art "optical character recognition OCR" without Bank B's business managers realizing that this was still a technology that had not been perfected.[1] They compared and contrasted the cost/benefits of hardware vendors, then summarized these for the client. The valuable "learning about technology" that occurs in the early phase of exploring new technologies, comparing and contrasting alternatives, was essentially lost to the client.

There was little or no dialogue with the client about the trade-offs of system options. Bank A's vendor had offered hardware that came with an almost complete software package that had years of testing and improvement in the industry, but was eliminated without debate by the systems integrator as not being "open." The systems integrator had negotiated a partnership arrangement with the imaging vendor they selected and would program the new system. This included the development of software for managing image commitals and retrieval traffic over the network. The bank spent much more for this software, which was an integral part of the software package offered by Bank A's imaging vendor—and had the benefit of years of improvement and fine-tuning. They also ended up with a system that was never configured to handle "real-time" retrievals (ad hoc retrievals were not possible; everything would have to be prerequested in batch mode).

Bank B's management had cut themselves off from the hardware evaluation and assessment of competing systems and vendors. All contact was through the contractor. So when technical problems emerged, the bank had no independent source of information. In addition, the vendors chosen for Bank B had no user groups. The imaging software vendor sold primarily through systems integrators and avoided direct customer contact.

B's Bottom Line

B's system suffered from repeated problems that substantially reduced productivity. The system limped along for months after it was presumably completed and turned over to the user. It was unable to meet operating requirements for throughput. Instead, there were delays, even stoppages, and a variety of unanticipated costs.

The mistakes made have common roots in how the project was managed, approached, and implemented.

- Enormous effort went into making a fragile new technology (OCR) fulfill its promise. This attention "starved" many more immediately useful objectives.

- The developers made little effort to involve actual users in planning or implementation. Users were perceived as unsophisticated in the early days of the project and defiant in later stages. Thus, when problems emerged, it was both easy and tempting to blame resistance to change. This shifting of blame meant that real technology problems often were ignored for long periods.

- In many cases, past practices were uncritically automated—that is, computerized. The systems integrator with an insufficient understanding of the business was not able to reconceive existing workflows in relation to the potential of the new system. As a result, much of the efficiency enhancement of the technology was dissipated.

Costly Technology Choice

Bank B left the choice of imaging technology to their systems integrator. They played no part in the decision. The integrator who had a financial interest in programming the system and a partnership with the selected imaging technology vendor rejected an imaging vendor with hardware-integrated software that made it easy to program workflow software to enable the user to customize workflows with minimal effort. Instead, the integrator chose to do much of the infrastructure programming from scratch. This turned out to be more costly to the client and, worse, created a number of unnecessary ongoing problems.

Consistent with senior management's desire to catapult the organization into the twenty-first century, the systems integrator sold the company on using OCR. Although this was to be used for only a small segment of the total document flow, its many imperfections and breakdowns forced the contractor to devote a high proportion of its programming efforts here. (Eventually, the client had to give up the OCR part of the system and go back to the more reliable bar coding that had been used by Bank A.) Senior management had no idea it was approving a high-risk technology. There was no hard cost/benefit analysis, although the integrator was paid to provide one. The numbers were plugged into a spreadsheet and based on little real understanding of how these savings would come about.

No In-Depth Knowledge of the Business or the Technology

Because the contractor dealt almost solely with senior management, it was not able to embody ideas and learning that had evolved at the operating level. It had opted for an untried, one-of-a-kind system that could not exploit the learning and creative insight that occurs with open interaction between experienced hardware/software providers and their customers. Absent was the kind of partnership in which the user is prodded to rethink how it is doing things and what can be changed and improved.

Prior to the push for new technology, Bank B had a traditional method of dealing with its the enormous quantities of mail. After each letter was opened, it was read by a clerk who then decided which work group it should be sent to. The new automated system in Bank B mirrored the old "by hand" system in which mail was opened, read, and classified. So in B's new system, all the mail was scanned into their imaging system and then "read" by a clerk whose job was to code the document so it could be retrieved by the proper functional group. This systems design created a large bottleneck.

The operation ran into serious backlogs. Additional delays resulted in part because the image system scanners were slower than Bank A's (at the time they were the only choice available for this "open" system) and because many useless documents were going into the system.

Users develop a great deal of workflow knowledge by trial and error, which Bank B never sought to uncover. As experienced users knew, perhaps 10% of the mail received cannot be "worked" — it was not actionable or required no work. Scanning and evaluating all these letters was pure waste. Worse yet, the system design had a clerk sitting in front of a screen pondering ambiguous mail. The system designers hadn't thought of the difference between working by hand and in an automated queue. There was no way for the reviewer to set work aside, rather than get "stuck" and backlog work that was easy to route. This had been one of the first "insights" Bank A had and immediately acted on. Bank B was stuck with this inefficiency for a long time before systems resources would be released (or were convinced) that this change was worthwhile.

In the words of Bank A's manager/sponsor:

> We had someone throwing out the junk before scanning and had realized by working with the system that we needed a way to set items aside (a supervisor review queue) so no time was wasted worrying a choice. We were also able to quickly identify the mail requiring speedy handling. Quick sorting of the actual pieces of mail into broad categories (before scanning) was much faster than pulling up items on a monitor and coding each one, one at a time. (The batches were machine coded almost instantaneously.) This type of sorting also allowed quick determination of backlogs and quicker remedial action.

The system consultants also failed to utilize the power of imaging technology to reengineer ponderous workflows. The best example of this was ignoring the automating of the adjustment process. The workflow system Bank B developed still had people calculating finance charges in their heads and filling out adjustment tickets, batching, spot checking, and proofing their work; data entering; and then proving and reentering rejects. The line manager involved had no idea the technology could even undertake this kind of job, nor did anyone want to challenge the manual audit procedures in place.

In an automated environment, these separate manual steps are unnecessary because the computer can do the calculations and update the account and all the relevant ledgers automatically. In fact, it offers a much better audit control by eliminating errors and providing detailed records of actions taken. These can be easily and quickly reviewed to identify any poor employee judgment.

The systems contractor for Bank B made no provision for this very simple workflow improvement. Users had not been consulted, and neither they nor senior management had much understanding of what the system could do. There had been no real effort on the part of the responsible line managers to identify and commit to cost savings. What savings were included were "assumed" and imposed (unquestioned) on the line management by the systems integrator consultant.

Another example of a failure to think through the application system in terms of the division's work occurred when the contractor failed to exploit the power of automated systems to create and print letters that would aid customer relations. Bank A found it easy to provide researchers with their choice of specific-purpose letters within the system. A researcher, handling a customer question, would be given a choice of letter and, once selected, the "system" would automatically complete it with the relevant "adjustment amount," name, address, date, and researcher's name. When Bank B finally did move to automate letter writing they discovered that their "open" architecture, in fact, worked only with one vendor's printer, and the printer had a very limited output capacity. In addtion, trouble with the (one-of-a-kind) print production software designed by the contractor created a major bottleneck in responding to customers. (In Bank A, the printing and data completion of forms and letters was part of their workflow software; no specialized applications needed to be written. Further, this "feature" had been developed after a great deal of field experience. New users were aware of this opportunity and able to employ it without having to have thought of it themselves.)

Most surprisingly, Bank B's systems consultants purposely introduced another workflow constraint. Perhaps fearing that their new storage/retrieval system would become overloaded if employees could order up any document they thought they needed when they needed it, their system forced employees to order *in advance* any stored correspondence. This may sound logical or easy, but it is neither. In handling service requests, the need often arises to reread previous records or correspondence. The most efficient way of processing work is allowing one employee to have immediate access to all the data he or she needs to completely work through a customer problem. At Bank B, it could take up to two days to get a required document retrieved from the system with their new automation! As a result, it was likely that several employees would have to reread and reabsorb the issues as a given customer's unresolved problem came up again in the queue. This was enormously costly, needless to say.

By way of contrast, the vendor of the imaging technology used by Bank A had confronted the systems capacity issues embedded in balancing image storing and retrieval in their large installed base. They had "off-the-shelf" software that handled this smoothly and effectively so there was no waiting time.

Ongoing Maintenance and Fine-Tuning

Bank B assumed that their managers, given their unfamiliarity with technological solutions to business problems, would not be able to maintain a new system. Outsiders with the technical know-how and resources handled the system even after it had been implemented. Programming requests were queued and changes and improvements were carefully controlled by the IS staff. Thus, in addition to being burdened with difficult operational problems, Bank B was slow to master the new technology and remained dependent on the outsourcer to fix, maintain, and enhance the system. Theirs was a very costly hands-off approach—leave everything to the outsider.

That was probably inevitable because a kind of self-confirming prophecy was operating. The line managers in Bank B, having been told they lacked technical competence, became increasingly timid in challenging some of the design assumptions and were always afraid they would be blamed when problems occurred. Line managers who did seek to identify system shortcomings found that their "data" was considered inadequate or ignored by the presumably more sophisticated integrator.

Reticence and timidity on the part of the line managers were then used as an excuse by the contractor for why the system's problems were not being responded to. They were accused of being defensive and not doing enough to support the new system when they complained of problems. And, indeed, the outsourcer may well have been convinced that the users were clumsy and unsupportive.

Lots of self-confirming prophecies created a barrier that made it difficult for Bank B to continuously develop and improve its system.

What Companies Can Learn from These Two Banks

In the first six months of installation, Bank A was getting back a return on investment far in excess of their original expectations of 25%. New applications were developed quickly with just a few programmers who worked very closely with end users. Management assumed that their new system was a "work in progress," something that needed to be continuously improved and adapted to new operational requirements.

At Bank A, there was no separation of interest between technical and line operations. And programming and administrative costs were modest. System development and maintenance continued to be managed by the initiating line manager. Ongoing hardware and technical maintenance support was provided by the imaging vendor, who was given an office and supply depot for its field engineer (who also supported service to customers in the surrounding area).

Employees felt their jobs had improved as many sources of job frustration were removed by the new technology. In part, this was achieved by involving those same employees in the design of the system.

Bank B's project was begun four years after Bank A had started its imaging system. Although A was located in the same metropolitan area, senior decision-makers made no attempt to approach them to learn from their experience. Bank B's management may not have felt the need for this kind of education since they were giving their outsourcer total control of the project.

Surprisingly, the new customer service system at Bank B essentially automated its old manual system. There was no real reengineering. Nevertheless, it was a complex and somewhat cumbersome system requiring two years to design. After implementation, problems showed up immediately. Bitter arguments ensued as operations personnel fought to prove that the new system actually slowed down service, while systems staff blamed all problems on ill-trained operating personnel.

Costs also spun out of control as the bank found itself increasingly dependent on the outsourcer to supply expensive systems consultants to troubleshoot and resolve system performance problems as well as support necessary ongoing development of the complex system they had developed.

By way of contrast, Bank A was able to reduce the time required to respond to correspondence and problems from fifteen to thirty days to three to five, a 90% improvement. At the same time, Bank A was able to absorb a large new credit-card portfolio *and* reduce their staffing requirements by 50%! Bank B's system failed to deliver even a fraction of the functionality and cost-saving benefits achieved by the hands-on, incremental development approach taken by its peer bank. There were no staff savings and performance actually diminished as a result of system bottlenecks of their initial system implementation. This led to poorer customer service and a continuing conflict between the users and the developer's staff. The users could point to the system's slowness, poor response time, and frequent down time. The contractor insisted that had employees been more accepting of the new technology, performance would have improved.

Bank B spent over $5 million on consultants to a build a system with the intention of supporting all aspects of credit-card operations from customer service to account acquisition to fraud prevention. The initial vision was much grander and more expansive than Bank A's. The client was inspired with the goal of catapulting its antiquated operations into the twenty-first century using state-of-the-art technology. They ignored a key rule of systems development: the simpler the better. Seeking a system that does everything is also a good formula for disaster, complexity of development, and horrendous maintenance. A red flag should appear whenever there is talk of such grand designs. The customer needs to "ground" these designs quickly by asking:

1. Where is the best place to start? A good answer often appears when the customer asks: "Which application is likely to teach us the most about using this new technology and system? In what application can we get the most back for our investment?" Usually, meticulously developed applications are more important than the sophistication of the technology.

2. How can we achieve the objective of having our own line managers not only learn how to use these tools, but to embrace them so that they become creative users? "Creative" means that the user is continuously seeking to improve and extend these automation technologies. (Regrettably, most consumers of new technology fail to give much priority to this objective, leaving implementation solely in the hands of IT groups or the outsourcer.)

Newer hardware and software (e.g., graphic user interfaces [GUIs] allow for extraordinary involvement of users and the custom tailoring of a system to their needs and preferences. A substantial loss in employee enthusiasm (and initiative) occurs when this technology potential is not exploited. There is no substitute for a sophisticated customer. Ideally (and practically—given user-friendly software), the customer plays a major role in designing new application systems. A hands-on business manager is needed to facilitate the satisfaction of subtle, detailed user requirements that can make the difference between high and mediocre performance. Many of these details are not documented—they exist only as tacit knowledge that has been worked out over time. Systems consultants need to interact closely with insiders to work through the intimate details necessary to achieve real effectiveness in customer service, quality, and productivity.

- Many managers still presume that user requirements can be embodied in carefully planned systems requirements. *But the user can't conceive of what it really wants or needs simply by careful thought and advance planning.* The best system gets developed in an evolutionary, building-block fashion. First the user has to become familiar with the potential and workings of the technology, then it must try it out, learn it, and refine it further.

- Mistakes will occur. *Paradoxically, seeking the perfect plan and systematically implementing that plan is a design for failure!* The learning must take place in a setting in which line managers and technologists interact with each other as well as with contractors. All need to expect and profit from divergences, tensions, and arguments. Too much harmony can impede creative problem solving.

- *When thinking about costs, it is important to do life-cycle calculations.* Bank B chose the contractor they did based on the integrator's analysis and comparison of hardware systems. Design and application development costs were separately calculated. They did not understand the "extra" costs they would incur by choosing to custom design and develop software that came with and had been highly evolved by competing "hardware" vendors. The costs were not really "apples to apples" and the bank, which had distanced itself from the evaluation process, never understood this. Cost comparisons are never easy, but by involving itself in the process Bank A was able to learn what these differences could mean to their business and operations. They were aware and concerned about system maintainability— and strove in their contact with other users to get some feeling for this. In contrast, Bank B accepted the integrator's estimates and completely underestimated the high maintenance costs associated with the elaborate system that was eventually developed.

Bank A's system was simple and inexpensive to change and maintain by its own in-house programmers, even though they had no previous experience with imaging technology. Further, its vendor had an active program of continuous upgrading (based on learning from various customer sites) and those improvements could be integrated almost cost free into the system.

Why Turtles Can Beat Hares

- Bank B had a "scorched earth" vision of a revolutionary system implementation led from the top by technologists. Bank A took a pragmatic, incremental view in which the lead was taken by a key user/mid-level line manager.

- Bank B, in "outsourcing" the management of the technology from selection to defining the system and then developing it, saw no consequential role for their business managers in shaping and implementing the system. Responsibility was turned over to the integrator-out-sourcer; line managers were given little education or voice and end users were almost totally ignored.

In Bank A, the line manager took the lead in building commitment and momentum for change from within the organization. The developers were also the users and involved other end users in every step of the creative process from conception through implementation and revision.

- Bank B management saw the project as "one-shot" innovation, a major development effort, which when completed would transform them from a manual to a state-of-the-art operation. The systems sponsor saw implementation as a "work-in-progress" — never finished, always changing.

- Bank B became enthralled by a technologist's vision of "state-of-the-art" and "open systems"; Ironically, the revolutionary vision ended up "recreating" the old ways of doing the job, with technologists modeling their design after a pre-existing manual flow of work. There was little input from line managers who had little feeling for the potential of the technology.

By way of contrast, A line management-led development effort had reliability and proven performance in a production environment as its more modest objectives. These goals favored the use of "off the shelf," well developed technology (versus seeking to push for the newest and most advanced technology).

Since both business needs and technology are in a state of constant evolution, it may well be a strategic error in many situations to seek to be the first with the newest and to do "it all" at one time.

A Final Note

By way of a footnote to this case, we suggest a controversial conclusion. Ironically, the rapid shift to "open systems" (mixing and matching hardware and software from a variety of vendors) can sometimes be the source of new problems, not solutions. In a "closed system," a single vendor (doing its job) meticulously integrates software and hardware. In this case, Bank A's vendor had worked for years to tie together scanning, storage, retrieval, and printing—with both software and hardware. Everything worked as it was supposed to: high volume, low error rate. Bank B's so called open hardware had all sorts of coordination/integration problems. It had great difficulty finding a printer that could keep up with the document flows and could not balance its storage and retrieval flows. The scanner was extraordinarily slow and a real bottleneck.

Open systems unfortunately don't automatically translate into separately acquired components that work well together.

In the next case, an overseas telecommunications company faced a daunting internal problem: theft of service by users. The solution imposed tough requirements on a new information system; the next chapter discusses how these were met.

Solving a Daunting Telecommunications Challenge

The telecommunications systems integration project we describe in this chapter illustrates how an astute client can develop an extraordinarily creative partnership with its outsourcer. This client knew that it had extremely demanding requirements. It was absolutely essential that the contractor fully understand and be able to commit to these requirements.

Certainly not every customer seeking the "right" contractor to develop the "right" system will be able to duplicate the approach used by WorldWide Telecommunications (WWT) (not its real name). However, its highly collaborative contracting strategy and approach to implementation provide a number of valuable lessons for any company with tough information system requirements. The detailed description of how WWT and its contractor complemented each other also supplies some important insights regarding excellence in outsourcer performance.

Background: The Challenge

WWT, a multibillion-dollar international company, wanted a system that would integrate with its other computer systems, never fail, and would allow for a variety of changes and upgrades without affecting uptime. The system would handle several critical business functions of great financial value to the company, including fraud detection. The system also had to guarantee 100% data recovery. (Their precise requirement was a maximum of two minutes downtime a year!)

Selecting the Right Contractor

A major requirement for contractor selection was that the contractor had to have a long-run commitment to their particular market. It, of course, was important for the contractor to have solid systems and technical expertise, but, more than that, in the words of the project manager, "They intended to force any contractor they would choose to prove that this wasn't a 'one off'. They had to prove to us their long-run interest in the telecommunications industry."

WWT's reasoning was the same as any smart customer in a fast-moving marketplace who sees the value of an ongoing technology relationship. One that would ensure having as a partner a company that would continue to make technical improvements in the technology they would be buying. *Thus, they didn't just want to buy a good solution to their current problems.* They wanted to build a relationship with the kind of vendor who would develop innovations that would update and improve their technology over time.

WWT invested a good deal of management time in selecting a contractor who met this criterion. Instead of competitive bidding among potential contractors, they determined to find the vendor who was most likely to deliver a product that would meet what they knew were very tough requirements.

The Extended Trial Period

Because WWT was a large, potentially very important client in a fast growing industry, it had substantial bargaining power. It was able to set a very high hurdle level for the contractor it perceived as having met its initial standard. And those initial conditions posed an offer that many contractors would find easy to refuse.

This is what the client wanted: WWT and the contractor would work as a team to jointly define the new system and the technical solutions to what it regarded as ongoing business problems. No money was exchanged at this point. Only when and if the design was accepted by the client would the contractor be given a substantial contract for development and implementation.

Obviously, this high risk approach (for the vendor) is not going to be a feasible tactic for most customers who lack WWT's unique bargaining power (or for contractors without substantial financial resources). However, what WWT sought to accomplish during this joint design phase and how it went about it can be adapted by many clients.

What Happens When a Technology Vendor and Client Jointly Design a New System

A small high-caliber team from the customer and vendor organization were charged with doing the design. In fact, each put their best people on the team. And both had experienced members with the clout and authority within their respective organizations to make commitments, accept compromises, and resolve conflicts.

Extraordinary Openness

As they worked together as a team, exploring problems and alternatives, they gained increasing confidence in each other's expertise. For example, as the customer recognized that the vendor was seeking a business solution that was optimal for them, they became more forthcoming with the details of their business. And as the vendor was able to learn more, their suggestions became better attuned to the needs of the situation. Trust built openness that, in turn, built more trust. Such teamwork was essential because a good deal of creative problem solving would be necessary for these reasons:

1. There was no "off the shelf" product that, with a little tinkering, would meet the client's needs.

2. The client's initial requirements were extraordinarily demanding. (One example: four completely separate computer systems were needed, located at three different sites, performing as a single system while appearing to the network as just four telephone switches. Each could not be down for more than two minutes in any given year without substantial penalty to the contractor.)

Unencumbered by immutable contract requirements and concerns over the implications of any fixed price commitments, the customer and vendor felt free to openly rethink—out loud and together—and rework the system requirements. In this context over the next year neither was inclined to presume (and thus to discount) that the other's positions were being shaped by short-term profit considerations or clever contract maneuvering. The team could thus obtain all the benefits of the distinctive and different competencies of all its members. Early on, for example, vendor team members could explain which of the client's requirements imposed undue systems complications and costs. And this was not perceived by the client as a way for the vendor to slip out from under some tough requirements or as a disparagement of the previous design work of the client's staff.

Put simply, there was *full disclosure*. The vendor felt free to discuss a variety of alternatives with their respective pros and cons (in contrast to "selling" their preferred solution or first cut). They were even relaxed about admitting uncertainties. They didn't feel the need to keep "their guard up." In the words of WWT's project manager:

> Vendors usually stress some sexy high-tech features and capabilities that they are all set to produce and that will capture the customer's imagination. They are hoping the potential buyer will get carried away by the "sizzle" and forget some of their other needs and potential deficiencies of the new technology.

Customers often get "wowed" and make decisions based on a buyer's description of some very appealing features because neither spends enough time really understanding the problems for which a system is the solution. Neither customer nor vendor feels they can devote "more time." In contrast, WWT and its vendor were allocating a good deal of time in this joint exploration.

Rethinking Scope in Light of Realistic Trade-Offs

Gradually, the customer began to rethink its requirements in terms of costs, priorities, and the time required to complete a new system. The vendor was able to provide more and more help in rethinking trade-offs as it became more acquainted with the operations themselves. And the WWT team members became increasingly open and flexible as their assurance grew that *the contractor really did understand fully their business requirements.*

For each, the favored approach was both cautious and experimental. For a full year they kept testing design assumptions and alternatives Only after they were relatively sure that they had a systems design that met their business needs did they turn to questions of size. How much hardware?

"Sizing" the Proposed System Using a Simulation

The contractor proposed that the client purchase several computer systems for the simulation. (The cost was substantial, almost 10% of what the functioning system itself eventually cost!)

The vendor would provide software that would simulate the functionality of the future system. Thus, the simulation would test the ability of the design developed by the joint team to meet the performance requirements of the client. One of the most important contributions of the simulation was to assure the parties that the system had been "sized" properly. For some very technical reasons, the client could not easily add capacity by purchasing more hardware and software after the development project. Thus, the contractor had to be sure up front that they were building in enough capacity to produce the performance required by the client. This also told the parties how many processors, disks, communications lines, and so on would be required.

A more typical scenario is described by the project manager:

> We were anxious to build the simulator because we didn't see things the way the typical contractor does. They just assume that if they misjudged capacity, the client can be talked into buying more hardware or buying a later model of the system that costs more but does more.
>
> We didn't play that game. By that time we were truly "in bed" with the customer and understood all the technological constraints operating on them and what they really needed.

One Last Hurdle Before Contracting and Starting the Project

Before proceeding to contract, the parties agreed on still another check. This was pushed primarily by the vendor. Knowing the customer's insistence on stiff financial penalties for failure to meet performance, they wanted to check out the design with some outside technical experts. After a suitable review of the architecture and design, the expert panel called into question two parts of the proposed system. It was their best judgment that these two subsystems should use a standard software product, whereas the design team believed these products were too slow.

But the expert opinion was taken very seriously and everyone agreed to some tests. The results would determine whether the design team's so-called customized approach would be used for these subsystems in the actual project or standard, off-the-shelf products.

The result was a draw. For one subsystem, the experts' suggestion proved better; for the other, the design team's original proposal was shown to be superior. Nevertheless the exchange and outside review provided useful input to the final design.

Typical "Games" That Are Obstacles to Teamwork

The teamwork that was created and the absence of the heavy hand of a fixed-cost contract helped avoid some typical machinations and posturing by the participants. These defensive maneuvers, to "hit the other guy before he hits you," work to the detriment of the final system.

The senior member of the team representing the outsourcer described destructive (to the project) "games" he had seen played when client and vendor were not able to build this kind of partnership:

1. Customers seek to specify broad versus narrow requirements. The broader the better, because this allows them to add additional requirements (that they forgot or discover would be useful) as the project progresses. Vendors seek to counter with demands for more specificity to avoid what they call "function creep." They try to prevent clients from learning as the project progresses. This kind of maneuvering is obviously not particularly productive.

2. To come in with a low bid, vendors often propose a system with the minimum capacity to serve current needs. This makes entry cost appear competitive while defering the real cost associated with any reasonable amount of growth, permiting the vendor to recommend additional expenditures for more capacity later in the project. Frequently, customers find that their new systems are outgrown almost as soon as they are completed.

3. Vendors have every incentive to design defensively instead of creatively. That is, they take the requirements specified by the client and translate them into functions that they have worked with many times before. They provide off-the-shelf, one-size-fits-all solutions for problems. If possible, they avoid really difficult problems that require a great deal of business knowledge and coping with internal group conflicts. And, as a result, they produce a mundane system

that doesn't do the outstanding job a more creative system would perform.

4. Customers learn to fear any changes in the original project design because it may give the contractor a good excuse to escape some responsibility (for cost or time).

5. Some contractors play "bait and switch." They show off their best, most experienced project people during preliminary discussions and before any contract is signed. After that, they "bring in the clowns."

Interestingly, in this case the technology contractor initially selected a third party to do the actual project management. This third party impressed the client with the quality of people it sent in to assess the work. But when this first team was replaced with what they called "third-string players" after work began, WWT threatened to cancel the entire program unless the technology vendor replaced the project management. This subcontractor probably did not view the contract as strategically important as did the one who worked so conscientiously to define systems requirements.

Obviously, these five tactics reflect a basic mistrust. Each side believes that the other party is eager to exploit them, given any opportunity. And, like night follows day, these suspicions or reservations make it unlikely that either side will give fully of themselves. Neither will come to recognize their primary dedication is to the success of the project, not their status or budget. Instead of being fully forthcoming, each takes various preemptive actions to protect its own financial position.

Conclusions: What Made the Difference?

This telecommunications example again stresses how important collaboration is on the original design. WWT and its contractor were almost off the scale in how much time, money, and energy they were willing to devote to jointly develop a systems design and project plan that would assure success.

To underscore their commitment to future performance, the client agreed to forego competitive bidding over price. And the contractor accepted onerous penalties should performance standards be missed. For example, when the system was up and functioning, if down time exceeded by more than 10% the contract specified maximum (a few minutes a year!) the vendor would have to return a substantial portion of its fee and refund hardware costs.

All the time spent in meticulously developing and checking the design and the capacity of the system reflected this astute client's emphasis on performance. The vendor knew that the real return was giving the client a system with the ability to function effectively, *not* a system that would minimize the cost of hardware and software. Any savings up front on these costs would quickly be dissipated by a system that malfunctioned.

For this application almost any reasonable expenditure was worth the cost, if and only if it proved reliable. The project manager knew this when he told us:

> I knew that if we installed late (missed scheduled dates) and the costs were higher, management would be upset. However, if the quality was super, that distress would be forgotten by the end of a year. But if you installed on time and there were many problems, you would never recover.
>
> Sure we established a time line, when certain things were supposed to be done. But we missed some of those dates and we missed some cost projections. But the quality of the finished product speaks for itself. The client was delighted.

One superb test of the quality of the work produced by the unusual trust and teamwork manifested in this case is the minimal amount of change requested by the client. In a system which probably contained more than two million lines of code only two significant changes had to be implemented.

In the development of any new information system, the "tire meets the road" in managing a project to deliver a one-of-a-kind system. Most frequently, that system will never have been built before. The client company is critical to the success of truly innovative application systems. To make the kind of contribution needed for success (instead of facilitating failure), its management must understand what these projects are really like. Chapters 12 and 13 give realistic views of the ups and downs and push and pulls endemic to all such large-scale software development efforts.

What Clients Need to Know About Systems Development

Why do clients need to understand the dynamics of the systems development process? Simple answer: because what comes out (in the working system) is not what goes in (as client requirements). Only a very inexperienced client for a new system would expect that the outsourcer's development project will produce a system identical to the one envisioned when the contract was signed.

The outsourcer's carefully drawn plan usually is impressive. It will prescribe what is to be done, when, and by whom. Thus, tasks are clearly defined and demarcated, milestones identified. And the resources are assigned to meet the schedule that leads to the prede-fined goal. However well conceived that plan is, because the system or process is essentially new and untried, there is no way that most of the problems that will occur can be anticipated. Although contractors and customers alike gain some comfort in believing there is a straightforward process (from the signed agreement to the operation of a new system), rarely is there a clear, unobstructed route leading to successful completion.

Automation changes the way work gets done, jobs are organized, and processes function. It alters the manner in which information is used, customers are served, new and existing products get produced and delivered, and decisions are made. Many times the implications for aspects of the business that were not part of the new system are just as great as for those being "automated." The typical new system design and configuration is only a blueprint for how the information and communications should flow after the new technology is in place. *But it has not worked before in this specific organization; it is untried.*

Plans Must Be Flexible; Change Is Inevitable

How is it not only possible but likely that a system that looks good on paper will have profound development problems? This can happen even when the client is using a highly experienced and reputable contractor. Usually, the contractor doesn't appear to be promising something that extraordinary, so what is it that can go so wrong?

Through effective project management, customer requirements and specifications get translated into a workable system. The key word here is *translated*. Although outsource vendors (and their clients) like to conceive of these projects as straightforward conversions of *the* plan into good, working software, that is not really what happens. Inevitably (and not because of contractor ineptness or perfidy), numerous changes, somewhat subjective interpretations, and trade-offs have to be made in the course of any development effort. And these will have ramifications on the final results—many of which will be deleterious to the needs of the business unless the client is actively involved.

Many of these changes will contribute to the disappointments discussed in earlier chapters, the costly crises described in Chapter 14, and some can make the new system almost unusable. On the other hand, the good news is that clients who exercise leadership during these projects can substantially improve the end results. The foundation for that involvement is the recognition that systems development is a great deal more than the precise coding of agreed-on requirements. An extraordinary number of decisions must be made during the development and in an interactive implementation process. And many of them need to be based on a dynamic give-and-take between the outsourcer and the client's organization.

In addition to erroneous preconceptions of what systems development is all about, clients can fail to understand how projects get launched and evolve in anything but a straight line. Those inevitable struggles and crises focus on the critical role of the outsourcer's chosen project manager.

Client Illusions and Contractor Delusions

Clients are going to take responsibility for this involvement only when they have some realistic understanding of the dynamics of these projects and why their participation is critical. After selecting an outsourcer and finalizing the contract, too many managers who have been involved in the planning phase assume that they will have only a minimal (or no) role as the applications are developed. Old habits of a mainframe environment die hard: "throwing the specs over the wall" and waiting to see what comes back.

Wishful Thinking

After all, clients usually have engaged in an often lengthy cost/ benefit study, worked through what they wanted a new system to accomplish, defined specific requirements, and negotiated a contract that holds a carefully selected contractor accountable. Now it is tempting and a relief to step back and let the specialists do what they are being paid to do.

Naïve clients for new systems really believe that by purchasing the services of a well-regarded systems integrator, they have relieved themselves of responsibility. They think their job ends with planning and approving the project and negotiating a reassuringly tough contract (often with financial penalties for inadequate functionality and delays). But every new system development effort is going to be marred by unanticipated changes, delays, and crises. Some will occur because of vendor mistakes or failure to perform by subcontractors; others stem from client changes or inadequacies. Still others have their roots in technology glitches or mistaken assumptions or interpretations. Often these are blamed on poor design, poor requirements, or just poor planning.

More often, the real cause is that there are so many inevitable ambiguities, even "blank spaces," in the original specifications.

There is a constant need during the project development to review and clarify, to seek new solutions and resolutions, as problems arise. The actual pathway from project inception through acceptance testing is tortured and twisted. (Chapter 14 deals with the most wrenching and dangerous kinds of crises that can either make or break a project.) To be realistic, this is what every project is like that seeks to accomplish something that hasn't been done before.

Critical Parameters Reshaped in the Development Process

The actual project that seeks to transform client objectives into a useful information system almost always turns out to be a period of discovery. Outsourcer and client both learn things they didn't know or conveniently forgot during the contracting period. How these "surprises" are handled really determines what kind of system gets developed—more than the original conceptions and formal agreements.

Client Discoveries

In a well-run project, users within the client organization will begin to see and experience aspects of this new system in some of its early stages of development. As they encounter some of the reality, they will inevitably discover significant omissions—functionality they need or constraints that they failed to anticipate. They will also be discovering things they thought they wanted that are useless or even injurious to existing procedures. And, on big projects that run for many years, the client's needs will be evolving with changed markets, methods, and products and even organization.

Contractor Discoveries

Given the computational power of modern equipment, clients feel free to require extraordinary performance. To support their promises, the contractor may understate the profound difficulty of meeting those requirements.

> A major financial institution had an enormously varied and ever-changing portfolio of one kind of security that was quite difficult to price with any degree of precision. The client had previously developed a confidential, extraordinarily complex formula to do this pricing. This system gave them a very profitable advantage in daily trading, but was designed on a stand-alone PC. They wanted a contractor to provide this functionality as part of their transaction-based host system. The complexity of the calculations and data manipulation, however, proved too complex to embed in the existing host. After four years of effort, the contractor was ready to admit defeat.[1]

Today's large client/server-based systems usually involve complex interdependency among an amalgam of independently developed hardware and software. Although widely advertised as "open" and compatible, the lacing together of thousands of embedded interfaces into a perfectly interlocked system represents a formidable challenge under the best of circumstances. (Most systems integration project managers recognize that so-called open systems still require an enormous amount of effort in integration.) Thus, some of what the contractor promised, probably in good faith, will turn out to be impossible to achieve or nearly so. These unanticipated obstacles will require replanning and work-arounds.

For their part, the contractor will also be gaining new information. Some of the programming they agreed to do and presumed they could accomplish may be extraordinarily difficult, costly, and even unattainable. At times, a promised hardware enhancement doesn't materialize from the vendor or a promise by a subcontractor that they were close to delivering improved software proves inaccurate. When a client is actively involved, the outsourcer is going to discover that some of the assumptions made or the interpretations given to specified needs are inaccurate.

There is a sunny side to all of this. Alert and flexible contractors will often be able to spot unforeseen breakthroughs that can provide superior performance than was specified and/or lower costs.

But that depends on the ability of everyone concerned to show flexibility and depart from the prescribed route.

How Robust Will the System Be?

Some outputs of systems development have much more importance to the client than may have been anticipated. Critical payoffs of a good system come from its *robustness*, not just its functionality. Clients want (or should want) systems that are relatively easy for their own staff (or an outsourcer's) to maintain and enhance. Maintainibility at a cost and level of simplicity that the client organization can support is always more critical than presumed. If maintenance is to be outsourced, this requirement is just as important, if not more so. If the system is too complex, the outsourcer will find itself burdened with the challenges of just making the system work, and will have little or no time for satisfying the user's inevitable need for ongoing improvements.

When under pressure, programmers can produce needlessly complicated and/or poorly documented code. Inadequate testing, sometimes the product of excessive project pressures, will also fail to expose bugs. Even with normal testing, the client will inherit the residue of poor programming. There can be many glitches that won't show themselves during typical testing procedures, but only emerge in day-to-day usage. Clients must keep in mind that there is a great difference between the typical systems test and testing the system in a realistic "production mode."

Mistakes made in the early stages through carelessness or haste *always* come back to haunt the project in later stages (creating crises of confidence and performance). One experienced project manager used the following rule of thumb for valuing the early identification of errors:

> An early mistake can cost one hundred times as much to fix near the end of a project (and imagine the delay this can cause) and a thousand times as much to fix after the new system is deployed by the client!

The Real *Dimensions of the New System*

The system being developed by the outsourcer is never the total system; it fits into a larger system and organization of data sources and work processes that must be interconnected to gain effective performance. This broader system includes policies, procedures (documented and, more often than not, undocumented), ways of coordinating, making decisions, and interacting with customers and each other. Making sure that the system works for the people who will use it but are not daily involved in its design and programming is in fact the much more difficult and often neglected project management problem. How human and machine processes come together is the greatest challenge. It is not over when the project design is finished and systems specifications have been written.

When a new computer system is introduced or changed, it inevitably affects the way work gets done. It changes the human interface not only with computers but with customers, suppliers, and so on. The consequences of these changes are often unknown and can't be realized until the system is used and the people using it become accustomed to it and figure out how to use it better. These alterations and adjustments are necessary if the system is to function effectively (or at all). Yet most system development projects keep the user out until the end. Somehow it is presumed that the easiest part of the job is the act of using the system. The consequences will be felt in every aspect of the system's utility and performance. How well it meets user needs involves both real factors and perceptions. If users are part of the process, their perceptions and expectations of the system are more apt to be positive and congruent. If they gain some experience with the system before and *during* development, they are invaluable resources for testing the project team's understanding (interpretations of specifications and priorities) and assumptions.

One of the biggest unknowns of any program is how people will use it—what seems clear and unambiguous to programmers in their design of the human interface nearly always produces surprises. People are not predictable, nor are the clients' customers. Uncovering these surprises as early as possible is essential. We will talk more about some of the project manager techniques—staging and organizing project phases and using prototypes and graphic user interfaces tools to get an early understanding of the human interface and system utility—in Chapter 13.

Programmers Inevitably Make Decisions That Change the System

As programmers translate requirements and specifications into actual code, they must make choices and trade-offs. An example serves as an illustration:

> In converting a credit-card system, a programmer noted that there was a tight constraint on the number of spaces for the card holder's name on the new system. The programmer decided to develop a small subprogram that would automatically (in accordance with some simple rules she devised) shorten names that required more than fourteen spaces. The card issuer discovered this choice many months later after new cards had been generated. At that point many customers were outraged with what the "name scalpel" had done to their sacred family name and sometimes their title.

Ideally, programmers balance the needs of users with what seems feasible. When isolated and lacking real insight into the needs of the client or an overview of the entire projected system, programmers can make "micro decisions" that injure the system in use. Here is an example:

> While working on a difficult customer information system, a programmer observed that it took three seconds to bring together information from two host screens and create a new visual display. The data from those two screens fulfilled 90% of the client's information needs when dealing with customer inquiries. However, the system specifications called for additional data that could only be provided if two extra host screens were retrieved. With a little experimentation, the programmer found that an additional 10% of data quadrupled retrieval time.

The programming manager responsible, however, decided to ignore this timing difference and adhered to the original specs without consulting the client. She didn't appreciate that for this particular business operation speed of retrieval was the most important factor. The user found the resulting system useless due to its slow retrieval time, and the program had to be rewritten sacrificing the extra information from the main screen.

Obviously, the client discovered too late that programmers are not simply coding machines; they need to be informed about business priorities.

Project Inception and Structure

The Systems Architect

Fortunate is the client whose outsourcer has selected an expert systems architect. These high-level professionals are the designers who structure the project. It is their vision that helps translate the project's objectives into a workable conceptual design. They make the critical decisions on hardware and software as well as how the total system is broken up (organized) into more manageable semi-autonomous segments. In many larger projects they are the indispensable "artists" who can translate the client's needs into a workable system design. Their knowledge of both hardware and software and how to integrate them to achieve efficiency as well as speed and accuracy is critical to the initial design. And they are often called on at critical junctures throughout the project to assess and reassess the design, technical feasibility, and trouble shoot performance (speed and responsiveness) problems. Clients must get to know these highly skilled professionals. Their experience, wisdom and candor often provide priceless counsel.

Architects will also define the interfaces among project pieces and often phase in the deliverables. Because of their high skill and status, architects are often highly independent, even outspoken. Wise clients sometimes use the architect's knowledge and personal courage to gain reasonably independent assessments of how work is progressing and what risks are emerging.

Project Launch: Realizing That Dessert Always Comes Late in the Meal

Inexperienced executives expect a "good" project to get off to a flying start with the proverbial bang. Overnight, programmers will be at work beginning to turn out "product." Regrettably, many projects start in a pressureful context: "We're already behind and we've got to make up the time and quickly." Such functions as project team training and team development can be shortchanged.

As we have repeatedly stressed, the time required for in-depth learning is consistently underestimated. No matter how good or prestigious the outsource contractor, it will not have the intimate, detailed understanding of how your organization operates or your customers and business. Lots of assumptions are being made based on formal documents like an RFP. Just as serious, most of the assigned programmers are brand new to the project and are not given a good overview of the how the total system is supposed to work—they know only the small part to which they have been assigned.

Serious students of programming are aware of this issue. A highly regarded, careful study of the problems inherent in large software development projects, after interviewing many project participants, concluded:

1. The time estimated for a new project assignee to become productive ranged from six months to a year.

2. Projects should begin with an extended meeting between the client and the customer. For several days the project manager, the architect, and the senior programmers should interact with carefully selected business and user managers. It will be their job to consider a range of technical and functional options. Next they need to hammer out a consensus on how the rather general, if not vague, objectives that formed the basis of the contract get translated into relatively unambiguous, detailed requirements.

3. "Writing code isn't the problem, understanding the problem is the problem."

4. "[Traditionally] the most important thing you could have was somebody who knew the operating system internals. We're now making the transition to (recognizing) the most important thing is understanding the application."[2]

Conclusion

As we have suggested, new information systems get developed by a torturous process, including a reasonable amount of failure. The original contract and specifications do *not* provide a clear road map that a development team can follow to a new system that will please the client, work well, be easily maintained and changed, and rarely "crash."

The results depend more on the quality of the people engaged in the development and the willingness of the client to be actively involved in a responsible, sophisticated manner. What all that means in terms of managerial action is the subject of the next chapter.

THIRTEEN

How Astute Clients
Exercise Leadership

As we have said, many clients understate the extraordinary challenges asssociated with the development of many ambitious software systems. Almost all new designs, no matter how meticulously prescribed they appear, contain a substantial number of uncertainties. Not surprisingly, this allows ad hoc decisions to be made made during the project that can be inconsistent with client requirements. Further, in the course of the development project, crises and pressures can induce some project managers to take actions that injure key objectives.

To obtain the information system that will be most useful, client managers have to be involved and become alert contributors to the project. Choosing a "good" outsourcer is only one step. Astute clients will also want to undertake their own monitoring, evaluating the skills of the project manager and the quality of teamwork that evolves. Paying close attention to the results of the contractor's Quality Assurance program is a powerful assist to that monitoring. Clients must also exercise great care in choosing the managers and staff who will be their representatives as well as participants in the development project.

Appraising the Contractor's Team

Ideally, the contract will have required the contractor to field an experienced core team that will stay with the project for its entire life cycle. It is obviously important to avoid a not infrequent contractor bait-and-switch strategy. The customer sees highly qualified personnel during the preliminary stages of the relationship who are quickly replaced by inexperienced personnel, often recent hires for whom this will be "good training."

On long projects, it is probably unrealistic to expect all the key players to stay with the project to its termination. Minimally, the client should expect that the PM (project manager) will see the project through, along with most of the key programmers. And many astute clients have the contractual right to select replacements when key people leave. (The contractor, of course, provides the names, backgrounds, and so on of available professionals.)

Appraising the Project Manager

Of great importance to project success is the project manager who is assigned by the contractor; this importance cannot be overstated. He or she will be absolutely critical to the efficient solution of the inevitable unanticipated barriers, glitches, and crises that strike almost every development effort.

An experienced client will want to meet and evaluate the PM before work begins. (And that choice may well have been part of the original contracting.) The client should assess the PM's relevant industry experience as well as interpersonal and communications skills. The PM's skill in explaining technical aspects to the client and understanding and conveying the business and its needs to the program team are critical to success.

Good PMs not only have broad project experience, but they know how limiting the more traditional "principles" of good project management are. They are flexible, good at early identification of threatening problems, and adept in working through creative solutions using the technical and business inputs of all interested parties. Such adaptive project managers believe that development is a creative process. They are comfortable with mid-course corrections and change and "getting out of the box."

Spotting Poor Project Managers. Their polar opposite holds on for dear life to the original plan and fears any kind of change. Ineffective project managers delude themselves into thinking that the tighter the controls the better, not realizing that change is both inevitable and desirable. Their failure to understand the inherent variability of these projects shows itself very quickly in their almost total reliance on computerized status reports (and a concomitant neglect of informal personal involvement and personal interaction with project and client personnel at all levels).

As a result of their focus on written analyses and remote control supervision, procedure-bound project managers are very likely to totally miss emerging, critical issues that should have been receiving their personal involvement.

Poor project managers are always keeping score. They look for "violations" to record on the part of others (the client, a subcontractor, or another vendor) that will justify a cost increase or delay—anything that avoids blame settling on them. They inadvertently encourage defensiveness on the part of key contributors: withholding information, sticking meticulously to the formal assignment, and always blaming "the other guy" for any problems.

The Contrast in PMs. In contrast, effective project managers seek to find constructive work-arounds that solve problems. They cast a wide net in building solutions. An example spotlights the contrast:

> An intractable problem on one very complex project was solved when the project manager brokered simultaneous changes in a hardware configuration with some software changes. Having developed good contacts with the hardware vendor, he was able to convince that manufacturer to introduce a modest engineering change on one of their relatively standard high-powered computers. Combined with a creative software innovation, this overcame the problem.

Such PMs also make heavy use of soft, informal information, as well as formal reporting systems.

PM Time Horizons: An Emphasis on Change and Improvisation. The focus of wise project managers is on a rolling short planning horizon. They are constantly taking short, quick looks ahead while envisioning the entire project. Their development plan is adaptive.

Assuring a Stream of Small Victories. A very astute project manager phrased his development strategy succinctly:

> The trick is knowing how to break down a large project. You want to be able to give smaller assignments that will provide programmers with a relatively frequent sense of accomplishment. These small "victories" give them the impetus to go on and tackle another daunting piece of the puzzle. The project team needs that inner drive and motivation.

Most successful projects are a composite of short projects, weeks or a couple months long, *not years.* This enables users to get a sense of the evolving technology and assess whether it is really "contributing." The feedback they provide the contractor facilitates the overall development effort. As each is completed, there is some rethinking:

What did we learn?
What needs to be changed in our plans?

A project taking more than a year before producing any deliverables can go drastically wrong without anyone knowing it.

Ideally, users should see a prototype of the whole system relatively quickly: one they can feel, manipulate, and evaluate. (A prototype is an operating model that seeks to emulate the functioning of a full-scale system.) This prototype is a powerful learning tool by which developers test feasibility and the client gets to actually try out a simplified version. This may cause clients to change their view of the system to be built. A classic study of systems development projects concluded:

> As customers learned more about the system's capability and understood their application better, they envisioned many features they wished they had included in the requirements.[1]

Successful PMs comment that they are quick to jettison solutions that don't work and quick to assess the ramifications of any changes in client business needs, well in advance of production testing and implementation.

Many speak of the value of prototyping and experimental approaches. The development plan has to take high-risk aspects into account. If possible, the programming is organized so that these are developed first (or, if that's impossible, prototyped).

Thus, a good project manager seeks to make sure, if possible, that the highest risk modules (i.e., those most difficult and most threatening to the success of the project—usually including the human interfaces) get tested as early as possible. How program components are organized and sequenced so that there will be plenty of early learning and frequent client interaction is one of the most important jobs of the project manger. A good project plan will sequence events (application modules) so that critical points of integration (with people, cross function, and systems) get tested against real data and real people. (That is where the client's team plays such a critical role.)

Monitoring Progress: How Much Has Been Accomplished

A project-wise client learns how to monitor the project. Traditional project management encourages common sense: comparing milestones with preestablished dates. Some of this is surely useful, but these simple deadline checkups seldom tell the full story, and they may even be deceptive.

A project that appears to meet milestones can still be in deep trouble. Testing may be shortchanged or even neglected. (It is not unusual to see contractors reducing the diligence of their testing when the project gets behind.) Projects that appear to be behind may, on the other hand, actually be highly productive. Extra time may be required in one phase to improve the original plans, which will lead to easier (and often) faster implementation or a more effective system, reduced maintenance costs, and transition costs.

Pressures that arise on many projects because of delays often encourage less careful coding. Programmers are discouraged from giving feedback or suggesting improvements. The result can be that a number of "land mines" get embedded that go off when the unfortunate user seeks to get operating work accomplished.

A broadly experienced systems developer made these observations:

> I've seen many clients deceived—as well as project managers—when staff report that they are 50% complete. Does 50% complete mean that half the software has been written or that 50% of the project is fully tested? Big difference.
>
> Then there are those naïve measures of how much code has been written up to a certain date. (A measure used very frequently, in fact). An astute client knows that often less is more. They would want a contractor who pays their people for doing less: using their heads to find better approaches that will make for a shorter, less complex, easier-to-maintain program.

Threatening problems are endemic to this kind of development activity. Only if the contractor copes effectively with these will the client get a successful system. This takes great skill because, as failure threatens, key participants on both the contractor and client side fear for their reputations or worry that they will be saddled with blame. As fears multiply, key team members lose confidence—and in turn these reactions serve to decrease the willingness to exchange information or explore alternatives that would involve modification of previous commitments or expectations. At worst, people retreat behind the contract long before any real attempt is made to resolve the crisis.

Teams and Teamwork: The Profound Challenge of New Software

Clients typically neglect to monitor the overall effectiveness of the project team. They need to assess its internal dynamics. Teamwork is perhaps more essential in software development than in any other kind of project. Unlike hardware, the elements in a program can't just be "fitted" together. The interfaces among components are many times more complicated; hundreds, if not thousands, of interconnections must work smoothly together under diverse operating requirements. Not only must there be a strong master design that integrates the disparate parts, but a closely knit group of programmers must continuously cope with the planned and unplanned interdependencies among their separate tasks. This involves a great deal of communication, exchange, and compromise. The craft of programming requires close coordination between team members involved in every aspect of design and coding so that each module will mesh easily with the others and with other software components and hardware.

Because projects never progress smoothly, a number of negotiations, improvisations, and joint problem solving are going to have to occur. Although some of these will take place inside the head of the project manager, many, if not most, should happen within the project team. One of the best measures of the team's effectiveness is how well these "micro-decisions" get made. In other words, the old cliche has a good deal of embedded truth: teamwork improves performance—more in programming a new system than in any other context.

On a good project, programmers feel themselves part of a mutually supportive, small team. Poor projects have programmers walling themselves off from one another or clustering in small warring groups. It is not difficult to observe where cooperation is nonexistent and great effort goes into shifting blame. (This is a temptingly easy game to play in systems development where an enormous number of mutual dependencies exist among subprograms and hardware.)

On one project, we watched weeks of squabbling over whether the hardware vendor or one of the subcontractors had made choices that were injuring the system's performance. Here is an example of the contrast when project mangers facilitate the team's work:

Smith discovered that some of the coding for which she was responsible could be handled in a way that would save substantial memory, but it would require that her co-worker modify what he had done the previous week. (These parts of the program had to intermesh.) Although it would require extra work, her co-worker agreed when he realized the memory savings this change would enable.

That is the kind of exchange that should be taking place frequently in a cohesive work group. And it is one of the reasons why the client must be sure that an intact programming team flows through the entire project. The other reason, of course, is that programmers keep adding to their store of knowledge concerning business requirements. Thus, a savvy client looks for these four "signs" of real teamwork within the project:

1. When problems emerge, key people ask, "What can we do to overcome this?" rather than, "Who is to blame; who screwed up?"

2. Those on the project give each other full information, even data that is not specifically requested, if it seems at all relevant. Problems are admitted early on to everyone who may be involved, not hidden.

3. Credit is generously shared.

4. Resources are allocated without acrimony and there is widely shared willingness to help others, even at some personal cost.

How Structure and Size Impact Teamwork

Clients should be able to observe that the PM has clustered the project staff into cross-functional small groups. Ideally, each group encompasses a subsystem or semiautonomous section of the larger system. This facilitates the inevitable trade-offs that must be made for their subsystem's overall performance to be enhanced.

It is easy to assume more is better; the more heads and bodies working on your project, the better and faster. Actually, as we have noted before, just the opposite is true. A sophisticated customer wants a vendor who knows the value of and can build tightly knit, mutually cooperative teams. Very large staffs represent a project risk.

There is a well-known generalization in the software industry: a really good piece of software is never written by more than seven programmers; a brilliant piece is always the work of one or at most two. Large aggregations of programmers lead to suboptimal programs. Unfortunately, marshaling a number of programmers is one way that system outsourcers use to show force (and, of course, increase billings). Clients must be alert to this tactic as a means to meet deadlines or squeeze in additional enhancements. Good project managers believe that this not only adds development costs, but can lead to faulty programming as well as compound testing and troubleshooting difficulties later on. Here is one such PM describing his experience:

> I was called in to fix a failing project. When I arrived on-site I found more than a hundred floundering programmers trying to make up all the delays and glitches. My very first act was to cut the size to less than a dozen. After interviewing everyone I weeded out all but a few who really knew what they were doing; the rest were a drag on the team's time. Everyone was always looking for ways to train them and/or keep them busy. Almost immediately, smaller numbers produced higher performance.

Experienced PMs believe that just two or three bright, committed people make a project successful. If possible, the client should gain assurance that the project includes several such individuals whose tenure will span the project life cycle. Unfortunately, contractors are tempted to shift their better people around among projects, which means the client loses their accumulated knowledge as well as the teamwork that has evolved. Try to discourage that!

Use of Virtual Teams

With long-distance communication facilitated by the Internet, Intranet, e-mail and Lotus Notes, among others, it is now possible to get far-flung professionals to work together. What clients need to remember is that an enormous difference exists between the kind of cooperation that occurs among technical people who know and like each other but happen to be dispersed and those who have never worked together before. Virtual "teams" work well when the project needs an immediate contribution from an expert who is not on-site. This is a valuable way to tap the experience of specialists whom the project could not afford to employ on a full-time basis. And such teams are extraordinarily useful in international projects that span time zones.

Virtual teams work less well when continuing mutual assistance is going to be required among strangers. Here information gets exchanged but there is no willingness to "walk that extra mile." Virtual teams can lack the informal personal exchanges that are needed to build trust, share findings and plans, or coordinate efforts.[2]

Being Alert to Critical Ad Hoc Decisions

As we have previously stressed, it is inevitable that unanticipated tough choices will be made during the development process. There will always be some clash of values between systems and end users. It is therefore important that a client advocate is involved to bridge the gaps and see both sides. It is the client who should be making the major contribution to important decisions and trade-offs between competing "values" or objectives (e.g., speed of data retrieval versus completeness). After all, it is the client's business managers who have a strong sense of the relevant business strategy.

Client Inclusion in the Project Is Not Automatic

Clients have to take real initiative to be integrated into the project. After the contract is negotiated, the familiar contractor personnel may disappear. The sales executive with whom the client had developed some relationship has now left the project in search of other opportunities. (Worse, from a client's perspective, other impressive contractor professionals, such as architects, who design or plan the project, may also no longer be available.) Most large projects, in fact, have a large number of shifting resources—

including project managers who get transferred to other more pressing projects or are "shared" across several projects.

High-Risk Outsourcer Temptations

Once the contract has been won, some outsourcers can also forget that they have a responsibility to keep the client informed and "in the loop." Many contractors feel their jobs are made easier—at least in the short run—by having absentee owners. Outsourcers can also occasionally fall prey to the temptation to suppress the need to rethink and reconfigure. Errors, omissions, or looming problems are sometimes hidden, glossed over, or simply missed. If project staff have no incentives to share and coordinate tasks, they will learn to keep their heads down, as much as possible, and avoid flagging problems. Even though a key programmer may discover that some of the original assumptions that went into the plan need to be changed, raising the issue can appear to be asking for trouble.

Experienced project managers know that most good systems are built on a foundation of failures. In any but the most routine projects, there will be a succession of unanticipated problems, even mistakes. What counts (and what astute clients need to monitor) is the ability of the project manager to learn from these, be agile, and quickly recover. (In Chapter 14 we discuss the value of learning from failures and the powerful new roles that project turnaround specialists are serving.)

How Astute Clients Cope with Project Uncertainties

Clients who understand these uncertainties and vulnerabilities learn to involve themselves in the life of the project in constructive ways that serve to preserve their interests and business strategies. These are the techniques they use:

- *Knowing where and how to intervene.* The client's team members are not "bean counters" or scorekeepers; they must be active participants.

- *Being diligent in communicating business/strategy requirements to the project team.*

- *Providing and supporting a client-based team.* Wise clients
  know the personnel resources that must be provided; they
  accept the costs and assure their commitment to the project. Committing their "best and brightest" staff will pay off
  manifold in a superior system. Yet it will be tempting to
  bypass just these line managers because they are the
  busiest ones. That is a profound error of judgment.

Communicating Business Requirements to the Project

Technology is a high-powered enabler. If understood and employed
well by business and line managers, it can transform the way work
gets done, customers are served, the speed and the effectiveness
with which decisions get made. Applied without that understanding, the results can be just as powerfully destructive. Yet systems typically are not built by line and business managers or end users
directly. They are constructed by technical programmers and analysts who often have only a vague understanding of the actual business for which the application is being built.

Specifications and requirements, no matter how well detailed and
defined, don't teach programmers and application designers about
the business. Nevertheless, from these specifications, applications get
broken down into modules, and individual programmers and analysts
begin their interpretation. For project personnel to understand the
business requires a great deal of involvement from end users familiar
with the day-to-day operating realities. The more feedback and interplay, the better prepared the organization will be for making these
momentous changes. And the more likely you will avoid learning the
painful way, from disgruntled internal or external customers.

Building the Client Team

As we have often lamented, too many clients embrace the simple
logic: "We're paying someone to do this project; we certainly don't

have to pay twice by having our people involved." Clients have to assign experienced, valuable people to the project. Availability should *not* be a criterion for choice.

For many, these assignments need to be *full time, for the life of the project,* not simply added to existing duties on the assumption that this is a part-time endeavor. Senior management must ensure that these "seconded" executives know that this is a tough, important assignment that really counts for the record and not a career side track. And they need to have a realistic view of the duration of the commitment required. These will be the critical people who are essential for:

Linking the project to the organization.

Getting required internal resources.

Making sure real end users' needs (and ideas for improvement) are being satisfied.

Becoming involved (or know who to involve) in the inevitable critical trade-offs; the how much *x* is worth versus *y when you can't have both.*

Client Sponsor

Senior management needs to assign one of its managers to take the leadership role in handling the client's side of project management. This individual is often the executive who conceived of and fought for funding for the project, who has both a psychological and organizational stake in its outcome (typically because it will serve an area of major responsibility for that executive).

These managers will have to confront intergroup conflicts within their own organization as well as facilitate or directly make tough compromises during the project's life. These difficult choices will often call for decisions that cause trade-offs to be made among competing client needs (as well as technical and vendor needs). Agreeing on the best course of action will inevitably require negotiations and compromise from a number of different viewpoints. Managers will need to have the psychic resources to persevere, rather than avoid confrontation. Many will prefer to distance themselves from these tough issues or cling to original specifications, however misguided, and avoid stirring up contention among client organizations who otherwise would need to be involved to make those tough choices. For them the organizational pain comes later, but the manager hopes to escape blame. The ownership the client sponsor takes and that person's skill and dedication to seeing the project through to a successful conclusion are indispensable.

> An astute senior manager/sponsor created a second office for himself in the unattractive basement quarters assigned to the contractor for two reasons. He wanted to be physically close to the project manager to assure himself that he was keeping informed and in the loop when decisions had to be made. This hands-on-management of the project served as a model to others. Also, he wanted his new office to be a symbol to other company staff that the outsourcer's people were professional partners.

Client Project Team Members

Key employees from the client organization should be members of the project development team. Members of the IS or IT staff (particularly someone knowledgeable about legacy systems if they are relevant) are prime candidates. Their selection should be made by an astute future user of the system: the line staff who will have to do the implementation if it is to be successful. They also should have an intimate understanding of the current process and a broad perspective on how it works within the total organization. For larger systems, the client should have its own team or "steering committee." These people will have the responsibility for facilitating the actual implementation of the system as well as advising on tough development issues.

Client representatives on the project team will become critical contributors to the continuing stream of decisions that must be made *during the life of the project.* They will be invaluable in thinking through the technical and functional options as obstacles and opportunities arise. They also have a key role to play in helping the contractor gain essential access to company resources required for the project: people, information, work space, data banks. They have an even tougher role of convincing others within the organization to make changes in policies and procedures that will allow automation to eliminate or facilitate work or interaction with customers. The project depends on various customer groups for aid and collaboration. Within the client organization various groups will have to furnish test data, provide access to and/or supply various resources, and schedule tests (that disrupt normal functioning). There can be a hundred "good" reasons not to coordinate.

It is not unusual for contractors to be blocked and even sabotaged by client groups whose power is threatened by the new system or who resent outsiders who appear to have more generous salaries. Without someone running interference, the obstacles these groups may create could handicap or even destroy a new system. In one infamous case, a mainframe systems group was able to prevent a new client/server system from going into full operation for several years! The cost to the customer created by the delay (and the internal battles) was enormous.

In addition to performing this bridging or liaison role between the contractor and internal resources, the senior customer project team members must facilitate the integration of contractor personnel into the organization. More than usually anticipated, customer routines will have to be intermeshed with project needs.

These project staff have another consequential responsibility: they should "model" the helpful stance that other employees are expected to take vis-à-vis the contractor. At the same time, they can help "acculturate" the outsiders by aiding them in understanding the values and behavior that shape the local culture.

Client Involvement

It is only through direct involvement with the project that clients can make the kinds of appraisals being discussed. Most clients rely on formal progress reports. As noted, these may hide as much, if not more, than they disclose. Invaluable to a client are these two kinds of information (which can only come from direct involvement):

1. Being able to predict, *before the fact*, that the development process is in trouble.

2. When serious problems do occur, knowing the underlying situational factors likely to be the source of the crisis.

With this information, the client is in a position to work with the outsourcer to make necessary changes or mobilize internal resources to relieve bottlenecks, change priorities, and adapt specifications—before events lead to a crisis. Such information also provides a contextual frame that helps the client understand the hard data.

Thus, the client must closely monitor the skills of the project manager, the quality of the team and teamwork, and the preparation and support they receive. When those observations suggest problems, the client needs to get involved. Sometimes it's useful to bring in an independent party to help the team (including the client) think through a crisis and reevaluate their objectives and course.

Ensuring Access

Many projects are handicapped by the limited access of both sides. Customers often insist that contractors limit their contacts with their organization to the formally assigned liaison personnel. As a result, contacts with real users don't take place. Important questions don't get answered in a timely fashion; at best, they become formalized agenda items.

On their side, experienced contractor project managers often talk about how much effort is required to both identify and gain access to what they call the "real users." They become a critical source of information on systems design when choices have to be made. The client often ignores this critical project need. And, regrettably, some contractors will seek to prohibit the customer from talking with any of the participants on the project except the project manager or formal liaison personnel. (Inexperienced clients not only accept this, they applaud it as good hierarchical management.)

Client Requirements for Access. Having representatives on the project team obviously should be of major assistance *if* these are highly competent and committed people, know the real business needs the system is supposed to serve, and understand what good project management looks like (e.g., in leadership and teamwork). But clients also need direct contacts with subcontractors if they are part of the project. Often unmotivated (and distant) subcontractors can be the source of serious delays and inflexibility. Although most outsourcers are not enthusiastic about having a client talk with their subs, it is only through these kinds of contacts that the client can understand why certain kinds of problems may be threatening the project's viability or become alert to possible alternatives.

> At the inception of the project, the client and their outsourcer agreed to use ABC as a major subcontractor because they had already developed a program that fit well into the new system that was being contemplated. As the project moved ahead, it became apparent that ABC was unwilling to do any adaptation of their program to fit into the overall system. ABC had been purchased by another software company and this project was irrelevant to the parent's current market strategy. For a variety of reasons, the PM had not shared this problem with the client. As a result, there was no realistic exploration of needed trade-offs to cope with this. A great deal of costly, complex programming was being required to work around the ABC subsystem.

How to Build Trust Between Client and Contractor in Project Interactions

The heart and soul of a successful client/contractor working relationship is trust—trite as it sounds. Contractor and customer team members must learn to trust one another and recognize that there is total *mutual dependency*. Neither "wins" without the other. Trust only arises out of the experience of actually working together. It doesn't come from idealistic, cliché-laden statements (verbal or printed) about mutual responsibilities.

Easy, continuing collaboration results from contractor and client members of the project team learning that everyone is following four simple behavioral rules of interaction. These are "rules" as articulated by one very successful project manager:

1. When I give others information, it is as truthful and straightforward as I can make it. No deceptions, exaggerations, or sins of omission, no catering to what I think they would like to hear.

2. When promises are made, I want others to believe they are kept; they can "bank it."

3. When I ask for help, even when it means the other person has to make some sacrifice of time or effort, I usually get their cooperation because they know I'll do the same.

4. People I talk to need to know that there will be no recriminations or punishments for the truth.

Clients can be their own worst enemy in this regard as these two examples suggest:

One of the reasons this project is in so much trouble is that the client has intimidated all our project personnel with constant threats. Therefore no one will really level with the client as to how bad things are going; all these technical glitches. The system is going to crash if we try to run it.

It is enormously helpful if the client allows us to be involved when later stage testing is involved. But now we have a client who doesn't trust us to be around when they are reviewing and approving the deliverables. We could learn things that would help improve the system if we were there, and also we could explain problems that appear threatening but are really simple to fix.

The worst of all possible worlds in running projects is when client and contractor communication breaks down. Instead of trying to resolve the problem, they get caught up in legalisms, trying to find the "culprit" who gets the blame. Much more likely to lead to quick recovery is a shared attitude: "What can both of us do to help get things back on track?" One then also needs to ask, "What can we do to avoid this kind of problem in the future?" This is where joint sensitivity to the dynamics of the project, its decision-making process, the levels of teamwork achieved are most critical.

Incentives to Encourage Good Relationships

Emphasis must be placed on maintaining a good working relationship. And there may be a need to build-in incentives. Here is one example.

> Alicia was the client's key participant in the project. She soon got "good press" with the developer by showing that she was willing to intervene in politically sensitive internal company squabbles in which future users disagreed over some performance requirements. She was equally effective in getting users to modify unrealistic requirements. As a result, her requests to the PM for certain changes were accommodated.

Mutual trust is an absolute prerequisite to communication and collaboration. And a good project manager and the major client representative on the project devote whatever effort is required to make sure it gets established.

Contractor Quality Assurance Programs: Their Major Contribution

Experienced clients have learned that good outsourcers have superb Quality Assurance (QA) programs. (In fact, their quality should be a factor in selection.) In these, contractor specialists who have *not* been involved with the project periodically impartially review its progress. They act as independent auditors and usually spend substantial time speaking with project personnel and carefully checking procedures, internal reports, and testing results. These well-trained professionals are required to provide very detailed appraisals. Below are a few examples dealing with project organization from the hundreds of items that may appear on a typical QA check list. (A heavy proportion will deal with technical issues.)

Do those responsible for systems tests have a detailed understanding of functional requirements?

Are client and server applications being developed by the same team in a single location, and, if not, have communications issues been recognized and addressed?

Are change requests being evaluated and estimated in an expeditious fashion, and is it clear who has responsibility for implementing any required changes?

QA is performed by and for the contractor, but sensible clients should expect to receive a reasonably complete summary that would include any deficiencies and recommendations identified by the QA team. These would typically critique the scope, schedule, technical effectiveness and organization of the project, and even the quality of the client-contractor partnership.

When clients do not have the benefit of such contractor sponsored audits, and there is evidence that the project is faltering, they should consider calling in outside IS and business/subject matter experts to undertake the QA. (A fuller description of the type of outsider who can be most useful is contained in Chapter 14.)

What Clients Need to Know About Development Projects

As we have emphasized, some key issues to keep in mind are:

1. Don't become obsessed with *the* plan and its milestones. Systems projects don't progress smoothly and in a straight line following a well-conceived plan. Successful projects have management that both expects and understands the creative use of mistakes, unforeseen barriers, and stalemates.

2. Make sure the project is broken down into small achievable tasks and that end users and client professionals are routinely involved in testing and evaluating these building blocks as they are integrated into the whole system.

3. Make sure project staff have adequate initial training and an overview of both the client's business needs and the logic of the total system.

4. Be sure that both the project manager and the client coordinator interact *productively* frequently and that the project team is working together and not losing sight of the whole (and the need to fit all parts together) as each member endeavors to complete individual assigned tasks.

5. Don't shortcut testing, no matter how tempting it is to meet key schedule milestones. The evolution of the more creative software requires frequent and thorough testing as well as adequate time and flexibility to revise and alter the future course. The impatient client will only pay later in costly maintenance and/or sluggish performance of the delivered system.

6. Don't just look at project reports. Reports can be highly deceptive, particularly in predicting long-run costs and business usefulness. More important is to assess (and intervene) to be sure the project is building solid, mutually responsive teams and a problem-solving approach that leads to creative improvements instead of quick fixes.

Thus, in all phases of the project, the client must be a real partner. Partners do not simply compare milestones to time and dollars expended and pressure hard when the balance seems unfavorable. They know that these measures are only indicators of underlying issues. And they recognize that they have to be continuously involved and share responsibility for how these issues are resolved.

Development Is a Creative Process Requiring Client Leadership

If clients are going to exercise the kind of project involvement required for successful systems development, they should have a realistic attitude about what happens in this process. Development project managers have to confront two kinds of profound uncertainty:

1. Even highly experienced outsource contractors and their project managers cannot predict what is going to happen when they seek to convert plans and commitments into a technologically well-functioning system. Inevitably, lots of trial and error will occur. But the process needs to be trial and error *and then change.*

2. And clients cannot predict all their needs and requirements in advance of seeing some "product" (as development is progressing).

Systems "evolve" as they are being developed. When there is no real partnership, it is highly unlikely that users will get a system with the functionality, enhanceability, and maintainability they expect. Having as an end product a system that will be cost efficient *over time, not just when the client signs off on the project* takes enormous client effort and commitment.

Ironically, many systems fail to deliver forecasted improvements because the project problems are not identified and resolved with users. Uninvolved clients never detect the discrepancy. Their own organization, compelled to get the work out, develops costly "workarounds." The system functions but at a much lower level of effectiveness than was its potential.

In contrast effective outsourcer/client partnerships often produce new systems that are superior to the original design. Motivated, creative participants have used their project experiences, focused by the energy that satisfying teamwork often releases, to find new breakthroughs and data handling efficiencies.

> Good projects depend upon teamwork, both within the project itself as well as between client and outsourcer. When well run, they represent a triumph of human ingenuity and persistence . . . and patience.[3]

One of the better kept secrets in this field is how many large new systems development projects fail to satisfy clients. Chapter 14 describes how astute, experienced outsourcer project managers can turn around near failures and push projects into pathways that are likely to lead to success.

Project Turnarounds: In Failure Find the Seeds of Success

Systems integration projects are profoundly difficult, highly complex, mission-critical endeavors. They usually encompass core business operations. Partially accounting for their difficulty, they bridge formerly compartmentalized business functions and existing systems and employ multiple technologies. Their objective: to have this integration work seamlessly and continuously.

The project team spans disparate organizations, and sometimes multiple cultures and time zones. And these projects can take years to complete—years in which they are likely to be buffeted by unanticipated changes in business requirements and technology. In this chapter, we want to focus on perhaps the most difficult and also consequential aspects of project management: the nasty stalemates and work crises that threaten to sink the project. They represent the make-or-break issues that can cause clients to call their attorneys and outsourcers to look for the exit door.

Why Are Turnaround Specialists Needed?

Because systems integration work has become so important to both outsourcers and clients, more attention is being paid to dealing with these almost predictable crises. They involve those high-stakes differences when the development process falters, even stops, because of an apparently insurmountable technical block and a loss of trust between contractor and client. The integration process has lost flexibility and the battle lines are drawn. Often such crises cause a customer to threaten to cancel or a contractor to walk away. The problem and the solution were well described in a meeting of experienced project managers:

> The most probable reason for the crisis is rigidity and stale-mate. One or both parties have become obsessed with making a success of a critical element in their game plan for the new system. They have repeatedly experienced failure in their strat-egy. The enormous effort (and money) they have expended, their sunk costs, have left them incapable of compromise or cre-ative thinking. As they feel trapped, they increase their efforts using the same approach. These are the situations that call for a well-regarded outsider bringing a fresh point of view, who has the skill to "shake up" the parties.

It is into this conflagration that some of the most experienced systems integrators have learned to insert their most skilled project managers. These are the ones aptly called "turnaround" specialists. At times, a line manager in the client organization also plays this role. These experienced professionals have learned how to rescue a failing project. They are the best of the best. They have learned how to spot the seeds of success in previous failures.

Learning to Take Advantage of Crises

Paradoxically, turnaround managers have learned that success is often born out of failure. A crisis is sometimes needed to create broad-based agreement that things can't continue along the same trajectory. This admission is the first step in honestly facing up to problems and making the changes and trade-offs necessary to move forward.

There is an openness, a willingness, as one turnaround project manager put it, "to try anything." This creates the ideal environment for change. The crisis thus actually makes turnaround somewhat less difficult than it at first appears. But there must be fast action before one or both of the parties seek legal relief and/or the relationship deteriorates so far that it is next to impossible to resuscitate.

Even though systems developers and technologists live in a highly creative and dynamic world, they too can be highly intolerant of certain kinds of changes, especially those that affect their work routines. Each group prefers to proceed autonomously, making decisions independently that may or may not lead to optimum coordination (integration) among the parts.

Finding a Breakthrough

Turnaround specialists know that severe, threatening problems, highlight issues and constraints that would otherwise be hidden from everyday view. Recognizing problems among interconnecting efforts, where assumptions, interpretations, and the different creative approaches taken by one group conflict or fail to mesh with those of another, often doesn't happen until craft (the art of designing and developing separate software components and hardware elements) becomes operational (i.e., comes together in the production installation). Identifying interface problems—the heart of the integration task—is thus made easier.

Because participants are ready *to try anything* to avoid failure, the opportunity is there to change the ground rules and come up with a new approach—to innovate. Facing difficulties forces the team to re-evaluate the scope of the project, and its underlying assumptions and break away from rigidly enforcing compliance with the original specifications.

Turnaround managers are able to reconfigure and rebalance decision making and project relationships. The objective is to create greater collaboration in the often neglected interface between end users and development partners. Here is where new breakthroughs can be achieved.

A Case Example. In some cases, the unforeseen benefits of the new solution can more than offset the initial setbacks.

In Bank A (described in Chapter 10) a customer service operation was brought to a near halt with the introduction of a new imaging system. In re-evaluating the project, a key line manager realized that the new automated flow of work reduced control, worker understanding, and accountability. End-user functions had been redefined more narrowly and processes proceeded sequentially. As a result, productivity did not increase as expected; the costs of the new technology appeared wasted.

The innovation that the sponsor/manager conceived under this pressure—to break away from the long-established, well entrenched sequential process and instead automate the full process cycle within self-managed teams—brought enormous unforeseen cost-saving benefits in quality, error reduction, and ease of training. But the greatest payoff came from the morale and motivation gains achieved with increased cooperation and sense of control.

What Happens When the Parties Open Up to Each Other. New technical solutions can also result, as the "firefighter" opens a dialogue among parties where project bottlenecks and technical dead-ends are admitted to and resolved. Teams settle the vexing issues of who pays for error corrections. The project can be resurrected—sometimes using a new platform or incorporating prototyping and new rapid development tools to speed up customer feedback.

A major bank had contracted with its outsourcer, a security-system processor, to develop a system enhancement. The vendor found the enhancement highly complicated, of little or no use to other clients, and difficult to integrate without affecting the overall performance and basic structure of the core system. Production testing proved how difficult and riddled with problems the program was—and how poorly defined (and understood) the system enhancement requirements were.

A third party undertook a review of the project and proposed a radical (to the participants) technical change. Realizing the difficulty of integrating with the host system and recognizing that the enhancement was one that the end users wanted to use as a decision-making tool (that would most likely need to be regularly modified and fine-tuned), they proposed that a local support system be developed. It would interact with the host system, using new software tools to access information, and perform the complicated calculations needed to optimize pricing and security decisions. It would also forward completed transactions to the host for update and processing.

The new technical solution balanced the need for stability in the core system while allowing for a highly customized enhancement to be developed in a flexible, distributed system.

Apparent Crises Can Lead to Technical Breakthroughs

Although project difficulties are the cause of and provide the impetus to change, it is the ensuing search for solutions that not only rescues the project but often leads to solutions far exceeding original expectations. Sticking to the same ground rules is almost always a formula for failure.

The window of opportunity is short, however, and an action plan has to be quickly formed. Thus, the turnaround manager has a great deal of power—but only a limited period of time in which to act. As one manager put it, "The recovery plan must be quick— for the 'power' lasts only one to two months."

What Techniques Are Most Useful in Converting Crises to Breakthroughs

Two techniques were repeatedly used by project managers known for their turnaround capabilities.

Opening Up Communications Channels: Penetration, Not Confrontation. Putting communications back in order is the first step in the recovery plan. Typically, communication has devolved to, on, or upon an adversarial process. Everyone has given up; no one wants to compromise or listen to others. Game playing ensues, with personality differences and the quest for dominance becoming more important than the project.

The project team's tasks have become fragmented and remote from the critical end users who are essential to the project's success. As each group keeps its heads down, avoiding contact and allowing no time for give-and-take (and the necessary trade-offs), specialists become isolated, busily completing tasks that, when combined, are not likely to work together or suit the actual and "unanticipated" needs of end users. The turnaround manager has the power to break this communication impasse by listening carefully to client and project team members, clarifying views and issues. Being careful to avoid "gotcha" feelings with the team and a tendency to want to jettison key players, turnaround managers realize that knowledge is embodied in the people doing the work. They look to credit the project manager, team members, client, and developer wherever possible. Their principal job is to develop strong communication channels across job and organizational boundaries. Making sure there are good "translators" on all sides, they begin a process of mutual exchange of information. Often the turnaround manager brings together a core team of experts representing the interests of all parties to focus on problem solving and creative solutions.

> In one project, delayed and beset with what appeared to be insurmountable obstacles, the turnaround manager found a room full of programmers (many new and in the process of learning) competing for computing resources and essentially diluting the power of the small number of key people with the experience and knowledge to solve the problem. The team was pared down to a small group of key experts and client representatives who together were able to solve the problem, without the drag on energy and focus from a chaos of new recruits.

Providing Radically New Perspectives. The role of the turnaround specialist is constructive—to provide perspective, mediate differences, and identify any communication breakdowns. And, as problems are identified, to heighten visibility and responsibility for change.

> In another project team members disagreed vehemently. The contract with the client called for the client to assign English

speakers only to the project interface. The user-interface team, instead, had no English speakers, but all were exceedingly knowledgeable and expert in their system. This was fully discussed and the team agreed that the more relevant skills were there and that the English-speaking limitation could be overcome in other ways.

The "perspective" of a third party also identified what could have turned into a serious communication gap between the development contractor and the prime contractor. The contract called for the delivery of "test cases"—yet no tasks had been planned to develop them. The team had *assumed* the software development contractor would need to develop these for themselves and that they could reuse them with only modest changes. The software developer, however, planned only to do "test cases" for changes and enhancements to the system—leaving a large gap in meeting the client's requirements. Identifying this omission early averted what could have been a serious setback in meeting system delivery time frames.

Who Are These Experts on Turnarounds And Where Do You Find Them?

Larger, more experienced systems integration contractors may have identified some of their best project managers as turnaround specialists. They are not simply superb troubleshooters but skilled negotiators. To revive troubled relationships between system integration partners and clients, a special blend of skill is required:

1. A strong basic technical ability combined with a critical intelligence that can cut across specialized disciplines is essential. The specialist must have a high professional standing in the eyes of cooperating subsystem personnel, combined with a diplomatic rather than a "know-it-all" approach.

2. Sophisticated organization skills are needed to manage relationships between contractor and subcontractor organizations in a high pressure, crisis environment. These indi-

viduals must have the ability to move into another organization and persuade its members to take on additional tasks as
well as adjudicate the critical "who pays" issues.

3. An aggressive enough personality to crack the protective
shells of participating groups to determine what's going on
and what's needed to meet system integration targets. This
requires a "how can I help you" approach, instead of that
of a critic, to avoid putting people on the defensive and
covering up reactions.

4. A positive, constructive (not fault-finding) approach to
understanding the various constituents' views, finding new
solutions, and building a coalition for making the necessary modifications.

What Turnarounds Highlight as the Leading
Causes of Project Failure

Any study of system failures points to poor "requirements definition"
as one of the leading causes. This is not so much because requirements are deficient, but because the cycle of envisioning and defining new systems, and the process of translating, then subcontracting
and coordinating components (subject to further translations and
professional iteration) are inherently uncertain and dynamic.

Contrary to the beliefs of many corporations embarking on
these projects, system integration is essentially a creative and learning process that demands innovation and adaptive response. The
broader (and vaguer) the scope and the longer the delivery time
frames, the more this is true. Underestimating of the complexity
and creativity of the task is also the underlying reason for another
frequently cited cause of failures: insufficient management support. As both client and integrator struggle to reduce project uncertainty, the following "mistakes" are often made that further
compromise the project's chance of success.

Legalisms Overwhelm Creativity. Invariably, turnaround managers
find that failed projects have lost resiliency or never established the

strong exchange in communication needed to sustain business input and share ideas as new technical and business challenges emerge. Instead, relations between contractors and between contractors and their client sponsors can easily devolve into formal contractual terms with each rigidly pursuing "specifications" and deadlines. These attitudes are in part attributed to "fixed-rate" pricing against detailed specifications. Such proposals give (the client) a false sense of control. Especially with large-scale projects, you can't fully anticipate needs and requirements and will end up with a variable cost structure and a change control process that makes it harder and slower to move forward.

Frequently right from the start of a contract that is failing, there is lack of mutual understanding and collaboration. Too often project managers accept client "requirements" unchallenged. At times, it is because they know changes will occur down the line and assume there will be time enough to deal with client misconceptions and naïveté; at other times, their own lack of confidence in the depth of their business understanding will cause them to hold back questions. In either case, the presumption at the beginning is that the important thing is to *get* the contract, not develop a collaborative, problem-solving relationship with the customer. But this is the ideal time for fostering this collaboration, for it is the inception of the project that shapes expectations and sets the pattern of the relationship. As one project manager put it, "It's really very difficult to think of oneself as part of a joint customer/contractor team. The customer reps feel they're there to protect the customer. Also, the typical unreasonable time pressures encourage people to ignore the customer and team building. There's a sense you are already late."

There is no spirit of marginalism. Contracts are designed to reward or punish; they are controls that demand all or nothing. In reality, such drastic action is often not possible and serves to hinder, rather than aid the success of a mission in which both sponsor and contractor have been heavily involved for a considerable time. The legalistic spirit of such contracts is antithetical to the very essence of systems development, which is, as one turnaround manager points out, "all about creation." Systems development is at best an evolutionary process, one that takes a tremendous amount of give-and-take to create a system that is formed to meet business needs (and tested and retested against business realities).

Yet so many projects become mired in fixed-rate pricing, in rigid specifications, and in project "methodologies" that reduce project management to the sterile discipline of documenting and managing tasks against timetables. Even if it were possible to assume that projects could be "fixed" and defined so thoroughly and unambiguously that a team could concentrate just on task completion, the very nature of large projects' long delivery cycles would undermine this assumption. Business changes and technological changes, over the two- to three-year life the average large system integration takes, will inevitably make the original conception outmoded.

Real Users Are Often Ignored. System development and implementation bring about often dramatic changes in the way the business is managed—in the use of information, knowledge of customers, inventories, not to mention the reengineering of jobs. The strains on organizations making these changes, however, are enormous. In nearly all cases, the client faces serious problems implementing these technologies and often needs help selling and building end-user confidence in the change. All "change management" research suggests that people accept (and embrace) change best if they are a part of it—have given input and see the advantages the systems will bring about. As one manager put it, "The project team needs to work with staff that 'live' with the system. Otherwise, you can encounter resistance." Ownership and control over change builds confidence.

Why then isn't there collaboration (and joint responsibility) from the very outset of the project, prior to this kind of crisis of confidence and threat to the continuation of the project? Often with "failed" projects, working closely with users (not necessarily the client sponsor who may be a technical manager, but the actual business managers and end users of the system) is viewed as counterproductive. The fear is that these other parties will simply complicate the negotiations and destroy the appealing simplicity of a single point of contact. There is frequently resistance from the client as well. "We need to overcome many customers' efforts to keep contractors at arm's length by appointing one or two people as liaison." This ignorance of the customer will inevitably lead to the project's undoing.

Success Not Measured in Customer Terms. The only definition of success that matters is the customer's—meeting deadlines or delivering the system in accordance with specifications may not be synonymous with success. The following typical example of those differences involves a major police group in the United Kingdom threatening to sue IBM:

> A spokesperson for the Automatic Fingerprint Recognition Consortium, consisting of 37 of Britain's 47 police forces, said they were canceling their contract after *"serious and long-standing failures in the service."* IBM maintained in its response that *"the system works,"* claiming that more than 125,000 fingerprints have been matched since the system was installed."[1]

Although a vendor may well insist that it has met the requirements of the contract, it is likely that future business and reputations depend on satisfying the client. Customer satisfaction and meeting contract terms can be quite different.

The Hallmarks of Success

What failed projects teach and successful turnarounds repeatedly demonstrate is that, to succeed, projects must be managed dynamically and require constant creative interaction between the business and the technical team(s). Client/server technology and careful structuring of client deliverables are powerful aids for enabling the client to derive prototyping benefits and gain the flexibility to reevaluate at each stage. Techniques for creating a productive, working relationship among client, integrator, and contractor(s) thus become the key to most turnarounds.

Use Prototypes, More Frequent Deliverables, and Pilots

Many customers underestimate the trade-offs between requested functions, the capabilities of existing technology, the delivery schedule, and costs. To establish a strong mutual frame of reference and clarify terms and associations between different processes requires organizing a new process that will involve and engage the client (including end users) in the creative effort. A very experienced turnaround manager notes, "What they (i.e., the clients) think they want, they may not like. I strategically select a small pilot group to work with and set small, achievable goals" that require the client and project team to work closely together.

Often the turnaround manager prototypes the new concept or creates new deliverables (possibly scaled back and simplified) that can test and engage the user in giving feedback on the new direction. This is one of the best ways to resolve changing or conflicting requirements and test firsthand the critical impact of actual user behavior. The prototype must be robust enough to enable the customer to envision the exceptional conditions and operational scenarios.

Keep Options Open

Plan so that there is flexibility in design, including early feedback with prototyping and phasing (partitioning) so that a large-scale project will not take more than six months to start seeing how the system and its parts (hardware and software components) will work together and to test the team's understanding of requirements against the realities of the various end-user constituents. The process becomes one of mutual learning between customer and designer—a dialectic exchange that helps balance the job of getting requirements right and getting them to stabilize.

> A huge Asian project was derailed after two years of struggling with specifications that were out of touch with the practical needs of the actual end user. A recovery plan was designed by a newly inserted turnaround manager who forced a rethinking of the project objectives. Instead of sticking to what was a technically *"killing"* requirement of designing 2000 different GUI interfaces, end-user task forces were formed. With their practical input just 300 highly effective screen interfaces were devised. And the even more beneficial

effect: end users were actually excited and looking forward to the change—instead of feeling overburdened by having to make their way among thousands of different screens. By inviting user input, the design was simplified *and* the client was well on its way to gaining user acceptance.

Failure Versus Turnaround

Most failures occur in the cracks between systems, between processes or between conception and execution. Minor and major crises will inevitably happen in every project at these failure points. The more complex (in terms of the number of interfaces, end users, diverse objectives served, and the different technologies integrated) and the more innovative (involving new processes, even scaling up systems shown to work elsewhere), the more fraught with potential for failure. It is not always easy to recognize the danger signs early, especially when disparate activities don't get integrated until later in the project.

The turnaround manager learns to look at these "failures" as positive and constructive, and uses the crisis to introduce the flexibility and openness in relations among all the parties that are needed to contemplate new solutions and take full advantage of the learning benefits of failures. Recoveries thus depend on two factors:

1. Recognizing that in failure are the seeds of success. Crises create an impetus to action, which the turnaround manger directs at learning from mistakes and sometimes finds entirely new solutions. As the economist Vilfredo Pareto aptly put it, "Give me a fruitful error any time, full of seeds, bursting with its own corrections. You can keep your sterile truth for yourself."

2. Forging collaborative relationships between client and between contractor and subcontractors is essential to success. This may include developing a new highly interactive schedule and plan for the next phases of development, testing, and implementation of the new solution that will ensure plenty of feedback and interchange at every step.

Converting Potential Disasters into Creative Solutions

The turnaround manager must correct the wrong steps taken early on in forming relationships that are too rigid and fail to promote ongoing, constructive dialogue between and among technologists and business management. This relationship style needs to be established at the outset and maintained throughout the project's life cycle. The test of success the client uses should not be whether the original plan proceeds without faltering. Instead, it should be whether client and contractor alike learn from the unexpected crises and adapt and innovate. For this they need an open, collaborative relationship for the team to recover quickly from these problems and ultimately succeed.

Every Good Project Manager
Is a Turnaround Specialist

Crises are normal occurrences in more demanding projects; they inevitably falter and threaten to fail. Success is the product of project manager skills in using crises as learning experiences that encourage flexibility and creativity. Thus, experienced PMs will often purposely heighten tension and increase the sensitivity of the participants to the need to seek breakthroughs. They use well-honed influence skills to defuse conflicts within the team and between the development team and the client before they spiral out of control. They recognize that failure comes when one or another party threatens to exit or sue and everyone insists that their position is the only possible correct one.

At some point in a tough stalemate outsiders become very useful because insiders are too tainted by what has gone before. Hopefully; enter a skilled turnaround specialist. Before then, clients should expect that a good outsourcer will have assigned that kind of skilled PM, who will make outsider intervention unnecessary.

No manager needs to be told that implementing change is as important as initiating the change. Chapter 15 describes what it takes to develop this increasingly crucial management skill in the context of new information systems technology.

Managing Change: Transitioning and Implementation

Too many new systems fail or are not even "signed off" by clients because the users reject the new system as inadequate. An integral aspect of defining what is needed and how it could be better provided (by a new system) is thinking through its implementation. Management should expect that substantial efforts will be required to *get the right people to accept ownership*. Outsourcers have a major stake in this as well.

While outright refusal to accept (and pay for) a new system is an extreme, many clients have profound disappointments as we have noted in earlier chapters. Many of these problems can be attributed to treating implementation logically as the last stage in the development of a new system. (After all, that is where it appears in the typical project plan and flow chart!)

Users need to be introduced to systems and technology concepts early and involved in the conception of the new system. As soon as possible, elements of the new system, even when unfinished, should be tested in the context of real work routines. Contradictions should call forth suggestions from users as well as improvisations from the technology team.

In a well designed development process end users should start envisioning how their work and roles will change and begin to look forward to the improvements and potential of the new system. In the best cases, however, there will still be the need for retraining. It is not unusual for such implementation programs to cost 10% or more of the system itself.[1]

Unanticipated Complexities of Implementation

The transfer of technology is not like throwing a switch to turn on something new that has been added to the organization. Lots of problems emerge that deserve comparable management attention to that devoted to the earlier stages of planning, contracting, and development.

The Necessity of Incremental Development

Substantial time may be required to learn new skills, and, even more important, to unlearn now obsolete skills and ways of working. At the outset, employees feel "clumsy," then discouraged— until the new tasks become automatic. Their managers have to be patient, but they also need to recognize that many complaints have validity. There is nothing equal to the reality of working with the system to detect real omissions or errors in design.

Making explicit what system parameters will fulfill business needs is rarely a one-time or a one-person decision, although some companies and integrators seem content with that premise. A new system that gets developed in stages with periodic reevaluations of "what we are getting and how well that works for us" leads to more workable and acceptable systems than does the "big," one-time decision. A key reason is that needs, as well as possibilities, only become clarified as a number of users get the opportunity to try things out. Earlier conceptions get refined or even radically changed when new potential *and* unforeseen costs (as well as benefits) become more evident.

Just as important, in a world of dynamic technology and ever-changing business needs, it is very shortsighted to conceive of systems planning as a one-shot affair. The systems that process information, handle transactions, and integrate business functions, as we have said repeatedly, carry the very life blood of the organization. They cannot be hermetically sealed and allowed to become obsolete or the business itself will suffer. Users who understand the technology itself, the internal dynamics of the new system, are much more likely to suggest improvements and enhancements. As business needs change, they can conceive of what could be changed to adapt the system. If the whole thing is just a black box to users, sensible suggestions, easy to implement, become more unlikely.

A Consultant's Experience

Here is a successful example from a consultant's work files:

Almost every large retailer makes some use of Interactive Voice Response Systems (IVR) to handle telephone calls. Most look at it as a way of deflecting calls from agents (and gaining labor savings), but because they don't fully understand the technology's possibilities, they use it in a limited way for things such as routing calls and giving customers basic account information. but Voice technology can do much more. For one, in addition to "reading" information from a screen, it can "write" information. That means it can do transactions that service agents might otherwise do. And because IVR systems can apply rules and conditions to its actions, it can systematically evaluate a number of factors about the customer's account (and from more than one system)—something not possible in the usual customer interaction. Thus, for example, the IVR can be programmed to look at a number of credit factors (credit ratings, delinquency experience, the length of time since the last increase) before offering the customer an increase in credit, and then actually perform the transaction that will increase their line of credit. This opens up a whole new opportunity for organizations to increase their service capability. It is the line manager who takes the time to understand how these systems work—who will recognize these opportunities and invent new applications.

It is a major strategic error to presume that there should be a neat division between those who work the technology side and those who work the business side of an organization.

What Happens When the Client Takes Over and the Outsourcer Seeks to Leave

Most outsourced development contracts anticipate that the client will take over the spanking new system and operate it. (Terms like "hand-off" and technology transfer are often used.) Most contracts specify that the developer will provide the appropriate documentation (of what they have done and "how it works"). In addition, the outsourcer responsible for integration or program development generally does a certain amount of technical training as part of the transaction and hand-off. (Regrettably, that is usually limited to the client's technical staff.) Just as regrettable, most clients complain—eventually—that the documentation they received is inaccurate, filled with omissions and even mistakes. Often under the time pressures typical of most projects, truly complete documentation gets short shrift. Of course, this is a major handicap to the client's technical staff or anyone else who seeks to troubleshoot or add modifications. Clients need to learn to monitor documentation during systems development and assure themselves that it is not being handled sloppily.

When Is Systems Development "Finished"?

But life is not that simple. This is one of the most vexing problems confronted by clients and outsourcers alike. The client is faced with the problem of how to assimilate these changes, this innovative new process (and often this very costly venture). That is, they must now get the new system to work well and routinely in an everyday operating environment.

Looking over development projects provides a good deal of evidence that this transfer to the user is anything but smooth. An extraordinary number of project managers working for outsourcers recount the difficulty of getting clients to *sign off*—that is, to accept the project as satisfactory (and pay the final bill). In fact, handling the termination is one of the toughest parts of the project. Getting out seems to be just as difficult as getting in.

Who Is Responsible? When is a performance problem a software bug (properly the responsibility of the outsourcer to repair) or an ill-conceived requirement faithfully carried out by the vendor (but that in operation is frankly counterproductive)? Or is it the end user's fault—have they been inadequately or improperly trained or prepared for the new system or are they resisting it and its feared consequences on job security? A spanking new system that is handled ineffectively by users is not worth very much.

It is not unusual to witness major battles between contractors and clients when the system moves to the production stage. The client insists that the new system is difficult to use or has an intolerable response time or can't handle the volume. In rebuttal, the contractor claims that the user is ill trained or, worse, purposely mistreating the system. Any performance problems are caused by the client's placing greater demands on the system (in quantity or quality) than envisioned in the contract. And there is usually just enough ambiguity in the contract or the facts in the case to support each of the contentious parties. These disagreements can thus erupt into threats of legal action or cutoffs in payment.

To deal with the problem effectively, users need to document precisely when and how systems performance is being degraded. It is the end user who must carefully do the observing:

- What was happening on the system just prior to the failure? That is, what tasks were being performed before the failure?
- What other tasks were being handled at the same time?
- What were the succeeding events?

Such precise records and data—what are often called troubleshooting logs—aid in diagnosising the problem and assigning responsibility for required changes.

When Operational Problems Are Ignored. The project team can be defensive when it hears of end-user complaints and problems after installation. The client should expect a certain amount of this as well as some disgruntlement from end users getting accustomed to a new system. End-user dissatisfaction, however, cannot be ignored or explained away as a resistance to change. The client needs to pursue and understand the system impacts and ensure that end users are heard—they are, after all, the ones who must understand and work with the system every day. If they are dissatisfied, the reasons must be thoroughly explored. It is surprising, even with an end-user group that has been a part of a design and implementation effort, how quickly end users acclimate themselves and invite work-arounds to the system's bugs, problems, and slow response time. They thus learn how to live with the system's deficiencies. The down side of this, of course, is that these are costly in efficiency and the client fails to get the full benefits of the new system. Far preferable is having end users working closely with those who configured the new system to find ways of improving performance.

Early Cues Ignored. It is worth recalling the data in Chapter 2 that cites the surprisingly high frequency with which clients say that a development project was unsuccessful and failed to meet their objectives. Our research suggests that these closure problems are the result of a predictable series of management errors. Here is a typical example:

> During the development process there were usually a number of cues suggesting that users didn't understand what was happening or that little or no attention was being paid to the interface issues—where the new system has to interlock with existing routines. These should have encouraged some rethinking of the plan, but pressure to meet deadlines and avoid cost overruns encouraged project staff to keep their eyes trained solely on the original set of goals. By avoiding these distractions, they actually added to the time and effort involved to find and then resolve them later.

How Can Alert Management Head Off the Problems of Implementation?

The process of embedding a new system into the routines of the client organization can be impeded by a number of predictable problems. Perfection is expected and modest defects become an easy excuse for damning the new technology. To be realistic, most systems have embedded defects; they are far from perfect. Some may well be known by programmers working for the outsourcer; others will come as a surprise even to the project development staff of the contractor.

We have previously emphasized the importance of having key user requirements factored into the design. Substantially new, large software programs are likely to contain unexpected bugs or fail to perform as well as expected. The following are *examples of embedded problems in "finished" systems:*

> The HR staff of a large company discovered that seniority calculations for employees who had left and then returned were handled inaccurately by their new computer system. The company's own policies were being contradicted. Although this problem affected only a small percentage of employees, word circulated within HR that the new system was a dud. This demotivated staff who were being trained and using the system for the first time.
>
> An investigation by American Airlines into the crash of one of its flights (in Cali, Colombia) disclosed that the autopilot computer program used in landing had a previously unknown limitation. Instructions for entering the closest beacon site were ambiguous. So when the pilot punched in the designation for the proper navigational beacon to guide the plane to a safe landing, the software selected a beacon a hundred miles away. Then in heading the plane toward that incorrect site, the automated system caused the plane to crash into a mountain.[2]

The "Nits" Are Not Trivial in Their Consequences

Users need to expect problems and either the company IS staff or the developer must be responsive to these complaints. There can be a tendency to downplay grumbling or complaints as "resistance to change" or dislike of computers. To be sure, sometimes those who are most vocal in their accusations can also be obstinate or even opposed. But an emotional smoke screen is a poor excuse for failing to take complaints seriously and exhibiting a slow response to needed "fixes."

Negative sentiment can build swiftly, even irrationally, when management insists that everything is fine in the face of problems. What seems a "nit" to a senior manager may be something that makes getting work out impossible.

> As part of a major systems merger, two systems handling over-drafts were consolidated into the chosen system. The consolidation was part of a large outsourced effort and deadlines were paramount. The project manager decided to save time by bringing over only recent account activity from the discontinued system. This left the service area with virtually no on-line history to help customers questioning their balances. The accounts were consolidated on a system that could have stored the last date of account activity—which would have enabled service reps and researchers to quickly investigate past statements when questioned—but this data was not converted either. Without this information, customer service representatives were unable to handle questions or perform research in a reasonable time. They took the brunt of customer dissatisfaction as well as blame later, when management reviewed the poor marks it received from customers surveyed on their service quality.

Providing Help with a Virtual Organization

There is a simple, obvious, yet frequently neglected technique for heading off implementation problems. Responsible contractors often make provision for a so-called *help desk* during some months of the transition. Frustrated users can call a skilled techni-cian at the contractor's offices and receive immediate assistance when they run into some difficulty using the new system. They can even be walked through the appropriate steps. Really good sys-tems development contractors use the complaints and frustrations collected by their "help" call center. Such user feedback should suggest future system or instructional material modifications.

How the Newly Created Jobs Can Be Made More Appealing

If users are involved in the design of the new system, it is likely that the newly created tasks will be significantly *less* tedious and more interesting. The "grunt" gets taken over by the machine. The inherent flexibility of new systems, particularly client/server sys-tems with GUI interfaces, encourages emphasizing human engi-neering values. Jobs become humanized. A middle-level line manager made the following observation:

> As we were designing the new system, we spent a lot of time with agents, asking them how they wanted data dis-played on their terminals—what would make their work easier and more pleasant. We even had contests over who could come up with the most agent-friendly screen display. And when we finished, the agents had good reason to feel that the system was functioning in a way that met their requirements and reflected their personal inputs. That had never happened before; it was always the IT department that made those decisions.

When the Contractor Does Not Want to Leave

Not infrequently, clients are not prepared to deal with the complexi-ties of a new system. Some systems integrators (outsourcers) have learned to use this ill preparedness and the client's insecurities to extend their contract. (Of course, some contracts do provide that the outsourcer will handle ongoing maintenance and enhancements.)

Clients need to evaluate their strategy and whether it is desirable to give an outsourcer the equivalent of tenure—a lifetime relationship. On the positive side, there is some incentive for outsourcers who design a system to pay attention to future maintainability when they know they will be responsible for it. Contractors who plan to transition the system to the client may be less inclined to think of the long-range flexibility and diagnostic capability of the system they are building.

Beware of contractors too eager to make themselves indispensable. They are likely to be those who make the client's staff dependent, unable to fend for themselves—a common problem when implementing a new technology that is new to the client organization. By inadequate training and emphasizing the almost impenetrable complexity of the technology, these contractors may succeed in "infantilizing" their clients.

Many clients want to maintain and enhance the new system with their own personnel. In most cases, this will save money and have additional benefits. An obvious benefit is that line managers can then be encouraged to truly embed the system into their operations. And if it is client/server technology, these managers will learn to evolve their own unique applications and enhancements.

Excessive dependency often develops gradually. The client becomes so dependent on the outsourcer's knowledge and skills that they can't let go. Reluctant to let the project end and believing themselves unable to handle it, they keep raising new problems or even requesting (and paying for) enhancements that will keep the contractor's staff on board. The outcome: the client's dependency continues and the cost basis of the original development investment often far exceeds original estimates. (See Chapter 10 for contrasting imaging systems developed by two financial services companies.)

Doing Different Things and Doing Things Differently

There is no value in repeating clichés about resistance to change. Perhaps the major objective of any new automating system is that it should make a difference. Both managers and employees should be freed of many pesky, irritating, and relatively routine tasks to focus on what human beings can do best: exercising discretion and judgment, making decisions. Employees also should be empowered to fulfill many of their tasks in a more effective manner. In particular, their decision-making calculus should change. As an experienced developer of data warehouses expressed it, "A good data warehouse changes what merchandise managers consider as relevant information and how they make important purchasing, inventory, and distribution decisions." This is a profound change in how those key retailing management jobs are conceived and managed. (For an extended example, see Chapter 9.)

If new information systems technology does not change how managers (and, in many cases, workers, as well) conceive and go about doing their jobs, they will fail to reach their potential. That is why the client's employees must understand how the systems work and feel comfortable in using them. Otherwise, the full productivity and quality benefits will never be realized.

A system is only as good as its user/system interface; it is not something that operates autonomously. Regrettably, many client's IT organizations and even business managers fail to recognize this. When they do, the outsourcer will likely be blamed for the system's shortcomings. And they will have shortcomings, of course, unless the business users take responsibility for fine-tuning and problem solving.

Throughout, we have stressed the critical and often neglected role of user/line managers in outsourced information systems. The next chapter summarizes the new demands on management leadership and creativity that we found are now essential requirements for building effective systems.

SIXTEEN

Making Line Managers a Critical Component of the Outsourcer Equation

Information technology is increasingly user friendly. Client/server systems and networks allow line managers to both develop and implement a wide variety of cost-saving and quality improvement systems for their own departments. What happens to these initiatives when companies outsource an increasingly large segment of their information technology?

Even when a major portion of information services is handled by an outsourcer, energetic, adroit client line managers can assume major initiations in proposing (and even designing) application programs that will fine-tune the externally developed systems. The splendid flexibility of client/server technology allows for continuous change and adaptability in response to very specific departmental needs. If line managers are encouraged, there will be many opportunities to substantially improve their unit's productivity and customer responsiveness without taxing the core transaction processing system.

Protecting Line Managers' Entrepreneurial Spirit

The heart of the PC revolution is to enable line managers to design their own customized reports, computer monitor screens, data arrays, and analyses. (Formerly, these were done by corporate MIS departments.) For it is often software enhancements, sponsored by lower levels, that make the difference between systems that function, although clumsily, and those that are fine-tuned to precise business needs (and stay fine-tuned as those change). An astute line manager's "mini system"—which may or may not work off the outsourcer's host—can provide enormous improvements in productivity and/or service.

The strategic choices that senior managers make regarding outsourcing elements or all of their computer technology may inhibit or discourage these critical initiatives. Unfortunately, in many companies, just as energetic line managers are becoming more comfortable with and knowledgeable about hardware and software, some are picking up corporate signals that their system initiatives may be unwelcome. In part, this reflects the cost and coordination concerns of large companies. They see PC costs rising exponentially and worry that "renegade" systems are threatening data integrity and security. Outsourcing is perceived as a means of centralizing and controlling computer technology costs.

How Line-Manager Initiatives Can Complement Outsourced Operations

Many managements increasingly recognize the significant contribution that line manager/system users can make in gaining increased returns from automated processes. Some examples illustrate the profit potential of decentralized adaptations at the user level.

A major financial institution had outsourced substantial operations and systems relating to their retail business. In reviewing their anti-fraud policies, the bank became concerned with losses associated with credit balance refunds. Some unscrupulous customers had deposited large sums in their accounts with bad checks and then withdrawn their credit balances before the checks failed to clear.

To prevent these losses, a proposal was made to delay the release of credit balances to allow time for bad checks to be returned; another to delay credit availability on revolving lines, when a check had previously been returned. Both procedures had significant downsides due to their broad impact on customer service (and even revenue). This new across-the-board procedure was proposed because it was just assumed that it would be costly to make exceptions for "reliable" customers. In effect, the 99% of good customers were being penalized (by not having access to credit balances) so that the bank could avoid losses that might be incurred because of a small minority. Their approach was appropriate in a "manual" environment, but foolish, given the potential of automation.

A line manager, concerned with customer relations, took the initiative in developing a simple application program that would restrict credit extension and control release of refunds, but only when certain risk criteria were found. The service manager realized their automation technology (unlike a manual process or simple host interface) could capture numerous account factors and revise action steps accordingly. The system could also be adapted to produce a report to measure the effectiveness of these controlling factors, so that the system could continue to be fine-tuned to avoid inconveniencing customers, but taking steps where necessary to control risk.

None of this affected how the outsourcer did their work; the new program accessed the host system without changing it. And the client was able to limit the impact to only the 1% of the customer base that represented the greatest risk. The application program was designed and developed within the client's own operation at minimal cost.

How Companies Can Maintain Clear Policies and Local Adaptability

Large organizations in particular, have always favored fixed, general rules. Exceptions were anathema—they were costly and intrusive. But in a client/server environment, these same companies can protect their cake while consuming it. They can control risk and still provide responsive customer service.

Here is another example of line-manager initiative in an environment of centralized data processing and third-party outsourcing:

> A division head was convinced that service staff could not be trusted to use judgment in retaining customers. He felt they would be too quick to waive fees. The service manager responded by revising their front-end system (running on a local area network to interact with the host and visually represent information, perform host transactions, and track activity automatically). The system was redesigned to identify and alert service agents to potential retention options, based on credit criteria, account usage, and other factors. A specialized training program was developed to enhance the use of this system, employing the techniques that successful senior customer reps had learned to facilitate customer retention.
>
> The system was then adapted to track both the reasons for customer closes and the options taken to maintain them. Data was used to analyze retention rates (by offer and reason) as well as to evaluate the effectiveness of training and techniques used by representatives to "save" customers.
>
> By using automation, the group was able to track their success and gain feedback that in turn disclosed additional opportunities. Senior management, instead of fearing that representatives would "give away the store," were eager to encourage new strategies and the broadening of the authority and discretion of service representatives.

Another example:

> More sophisticated risk management techniques for controlling bad debt losses made it increasingly difficult (if not impossible) for staff (in a lending operation) to respond quickly to customer loan requests. There were just too many experience factors to evaluate.
>
> A line manager initiated the development of a small application program that made it possible for those dealing with new customers to take into account, in minutes, the more complex criteria (using their desktop). Staff were thus able to maintain customer responsiveness with *no* increase in servicing costs.

Employee acceptance of new centralized systems can be accelerated by line managers with some technology know-how. In the extended description of Bank A in Chapter 10, the middle manager was very successful in demonstrating to employees how they could adapt the new information system to their unique requirements and even preferences. She even got software that allowed customer service agents to "paint" new screen displays. This hands-on technique got agents feeling comfortable and creative with the potential of the new system.[1] The ability to change a system in ways that meet your needs is obviously an important element in gaining acceptance.

Resolving Interdepartmental Disputes

Interdepartmental disagreements and buck passing are facts of corporate life, and costly ones. They are just as apt to happen, and perhaps with more frequency, when processes and responsibility span outsourcer and internal operations. With some computer knowledge, instead of finger pointing, managers can use systems to help identify problems and resolve them. Here is a case of how effective managers can be when they understand and use the computer tools at their disposal:

> A bank had outsourced the insurance monitoring process for its mortgage accounts. The service provider had a system for collecting renewal information from insurance carriers (and brokers). If hazard insurance on mortgage properties lapsed, they would generate letters to customers to alert them before proceeding to initiate a blanket insurance protection. Service representatives were finding that customers (and their insurance brokers) were often claiming to have sent renewal information to the vendor, faxing these documents again and again. A number of procedures and policy changes were made between bank and vendor to reduce the amount of customer inconvenience, but the problem persisted. A line manager decided to set up their fax server and directed customers to send renewal notices by fax directly to the bank. The bank was able to store and identify fax receipts, and then immediately forward (re-

route) the fax to the outsourcer. This simple control made it possible for the bank to monitor how quickly the outsourcer updated their data base from the time the fax was sent.

And here is a case in which a large organization's highly specialized knowledge and compartmentalized management of its systems left them unable to cope with a crisis. It required a business line manager with a broader understanding of their systems to deal with a consequential customer service embarrassment.

A very large retail broker received a good deal of unfavorable publicity because they tolerated (for the good share of a day) the dissemination of erroneous information over their interactive voice response system. The firm had made some program changes to their host system. When the new software release was updated, it failed to include reporting from all its mutual funds. Customer net worth was thus vastly understated and the problem was quickly identified by distraught customers. IT management (not an outsourcer) was aware of the problem, but felt it was "safer" to make the changes needed at their next scheduled update. Meanwhile, tens of thousands of investment customers were worried needlessly when they called and used the brokerage firm's automated Voice Response System only to find their net worth had fallen dramatically.

The simple expedient of taking the voice response system offline or automating a message to ask customers to call back at a later time when this data could be expected to be updated was apparently never considered. The Voice Response System was the responsibility of another group (who had all the programming of the system done by an outsourcer). The service manager didn't know enough about the technology to understand how easily it could be modified to cope with the emergency. And the IT department didn't think about any other remedies (or system consequences). System responsibilities were dispersed and the line managers had lost control of a consequential part of their business.

Line Managers Must Be Involved in Systems Development

Chapter 13 provided a host of examples of where and why users, (i.e., line managers) have to be an integral part of any systems development project. Just to review some of these reasons:

- They are needed for assessing alternatives and the usefulness of early prototypes. "Do these work for us?" In the development of the successful data warehouse (Chapter 9), merchandise managers gave continuous feedback that shaped the kind of data and analyses that would be provided.

- Many programming trade-offs have to be made during the development process. These are more likely to be business enhancing if line managers are involved and taking some responsibility.

- Implementation is a much smoother process (and acceptance greater) when line managers are able to take part in the system's evolution. Systems then become tools, and managers learn to readily develop "fixes" or local application programs to cope with omissions or mistakes.

The incremental strategy that appears to be most productive for complex systems development projects presumes that users will be able to provide more and better contributions as they obtain more of a feel for the technology. This is real-time line management feedback.

What Companies Gain When They Encourage Line-Management Initiatives with Outsourced Information Systems

Empowerment becomes more meaningful when employees see their proposals embodied in new work procedures and job designs almost overnight. Client/server systems—if properly used and designed—can make the process of getting employees involved and accustomed to change as a literal everyday occurrence. Systems, when seen by staff as tools for making the job easier and more efficient, can become a powerful means of furthering productivity and morale.

Many line managers are just beginning to test the power and independence that new technology makes possible. They are starting to realize the vast advancements in productivity, quality, and service that can be gained from having middle managers engage in continuous "micro-engineering" by means of automation that *they control*. Companies seeking high performance are stressing "value-adding" managers (who aren't simply links in a traditional hierarchy). Increasingly, PCs are a critical tool in empowering managers to take more responsibility for quality, service, and costs at the local level. This cannot be done if systems outsourcing further distances staff from technical know-how and active participation in the application of these technologies.

Learning how to manage systems—and the sometimes thousands or even hundreds of thousands of mistakes one error may cause—requires concerted effort on the part of the client's staff. The more line managers know about their systems, the better they will be at avoiding programming flaws and embarrassing and costly rework. And the better they will be at using these "tools" to improve efficiency, control, reliability, and decision making.

But these kinds of effective improvisations and initiatives represent a highly perishable corporate asset. Gains are based on hands-on experience and the willingness to learn enough about these new technologies to be comfortable in their use and adaptation. Many information systems operate significantly below their capacity to deliver improved service and decision support. Only a sophisticated insider can push them to deliver.

Ceding total control of technology to outsourcers or reverting to strict standards and central control over new initiatives can stifle the willingness of line managers to undertake to master the intricacies of the hardware and software. Outsourcing operations needs to be accomplished with an understanding of what client line managers can contribute to overall organizational performance when they fully exploit the power of information technology.

Business Managers' Responsibility for Outsourcing Operating Standards

These same line managers need to be the ones who set the standards and monitor outside contractors. They are the ones who understand the subtle performance issues that must go into outsourced operations if business strategies are to predominate, not the outsourcer's well-honed routines. Fortunately, no conflicts arise as long as senior management expects this level of user involvement in outsourcing and recognizes the adaptive power of local area network systems (LANS).

For the first time, technologically, an organization can have standardization and centralization living comfortably with exceptions and customization. Unique business strategies and line-manager know-how can get factored into outsourced operations. But senior management has to want that to happen, understand its importance and encouraging the use of new generations of software that make these local adaptations feasible and economical. Today, business managers can customize business solutions with fairly inexpensive front-end application systems. This may reduce the number of standardized policies, across-the-board rules, and the one-size-fits-all approach.

Managers who are encouraged to familiarize themselves with and be comfortable with the technology side of their operations will reconceive many of the parameters of work and strategy. These imaginative and creative initiatives are what business seeks in today's fast-moving, enormously competitive markets. It would be folly to allow outsourcing and recentralization of computer technology to have the unanticipated effect of destroying those managerial skills most needed in today's world.

Systems become most useful and profitable when they become the tools of management. Then they are adapted by line managers who use them to improve workflow, increase service, and evaluate and improve marketing decisions. This serves to close the gap between conception and development, between idea and innovation.

Successful companies have learned to deal with the underlying paradox in outsourcing information systems. These companies have resolved the inherent complications of using outsiders to do something for which the insider must ultimately be responsible. Chapter 17 summarizes what companies have learned about broadening the skill set of line managers to work effectively with specialists both inside and outside the company.

New Demands on Outsourcing:
The Long-Run Perspective

Executives do not have to be told that their computer-based information systems have moved up and out from the back office. They have become indispensable to the management of almost every company.

Less well known, but hardly a secret, is the extraordinary potential of these newer, more powerful systems for transforming and rejuvenating managerial work by providing new strategic options and greater tactical flexibility and adaptability.

When customers seek a product or service variation or when supply sources undergo sudden changes or a new competitor implements an innovative strategy, alert managers can quickly mobilize adept responses. Even large organizations can transform themselves from ponderous monoliths to fleet-footed competitors. Their lower and mid-level managers can become key players by assuming more direct responsibility for initiating change. (Recall the many examples in the previous chapter.)

And new corporate market and product strategies are more likely to be based on comprehensive data than intuition given the vast storage, retrieval, and manipulative capabilities inherent in these new systems.

In the real world there are always "ifs" and "buts" standing in the way of nirvanas. These world-class transformations are profoundly dependent on the relatively new management structural innovation: the use of outsourcers to provide technology problem solving in place of insider staff.

We have sought to explore the challenges posed by this profound organizational change in how business operates. Our research identified several that were the most critical to improved competitiveness . . . and, ironically, also the most neglected!

- Devise and maintain a pattern of creative teamwork so that the insider/user's intimate knowledge of the business, its present and future needs, gets integrated with the expert technology capabilities of the outsourcer.

- Conceive and develop systems which can be "works in progress," that is, they have dynamic capabilities to evolve with the inevitable changes the business will confront.

- Use a technology development process that empowers line managers to exploit the flexibility and adaptability inherent in these new line technologies by initiating customized enhancements.

To meet these challenges, executives need both perspective on outsourcing as a process and guidelines to facilitate its use.

Everyone Now Outsources

We live in a technological age in which it is easy to assume that what appears impossible can be done—although it may take a bit longer. But the record shows substantial client grumbling about prolonged hardships and disagreements with outsourcers in the development of a new information system. (And just as much dissatisfaction with completed systems and outsourced operations.) Paradoxically, as automated information systems have become indispensable to the functioning of most companies and the day-to-day work of their managers, these companies are turning to outsiders to develop and often manage those critical systems.

With an emphasis on shedding non-core products and functions, information systems become a tempting candidate to outsource. Further encouragement to outsource these systems, if such is needed, is provided by their inherent complexity, cost, and volatility. These technologies are evolving with extraordinary rapidity and demand an ever-increasing body of arcane knowledge combined with the willingness to foot ever-larger bills for new installations and maintenance of what is already in place. It is thus not surprising that this spiral appears:

- Technology costs and their skill requirements keep increasing
- Greater use of outsourcing
- Internal staffs depleted and unable to keep up with new demands
- More outsourcing to make up for absence of internal resources

There are two not-so-hidden dilemmas here: (1) Information systems technology may not represent a core technology for most organizations, but it supports and is an essential component of what companies are about. (2) These outsider systems can't be built and can't operate without continuous, knowledgeable inputs from insiders. Without intensive and extensive involvement of actual users, the systems will not be an effective support of current and future management strategies. But senior management has been slow to recognize the limitations of the outsider, the systems contractor. Explaining the "why" is speculation. For something as intimidating as many of these information systems (costly, vulnerable, extremely technical) it is reassuring to executives buffeted by uncertainty to believe that an expert outsider can do it all.

Supporting this wishful thinking are long-standing myths about delegation. That is, the good manager doesn't need to get involved and perhaps shouldn't. Give orders and assess the final results—how else to be a "one-minute manager"?

The Needed Leadership Skills

Unfortunately, most companies place little emphasis on leadership skills in the management of outsourced technologies. What is to lead? Lots, is the answer. Managers must make the technology *their business*. Managers throughout an organization utilizing computer-based information and communication need to understand the underlying technology well enough to make critical choices. There will be choices at every stage of new systems development and ongoing systems operations.

Increasingly, a criterion for management selection will be the ability to manage information technology. As we have said repeatedly and emphatically, outsourcing does not eliminate the need to manage information systems. The more routine decisions can be made by the outsourcer, but not those that relate to business strategy and customer service.

An often-neglected aspect of that leadership is the ability to select outsourcer staff able to communicate directly and unambiguously (in plain English). Business managers need to comprehend the choices they have, and the consequences of their decisions, as they relate to the potential as well as the functioning of current or contemplated technology. They need to know what are reasonable expectations; what are the potentials they can tap for new applications. It is the insiders who have to take responsibility and make these systems "their business."

Partnering — More Than a Mantra

It is easy to forget that a complex computer-based information system is only useful if it works well in a real organization. A technically "correct" system that meets a legalistic definition of contractually agreed-on requirements can be (and, regrettably, often is) a financial and operational failure. To be worth their cost and fulfill their potential, these systems must have evolved and adapted to meet numerous "real-world" inconsistencies and contradictions.

To be sure, client reengineering that takes place before systems design can handle some workflow contradictions; others may get worked through in the planning stage. But most get recognized during the actual development and implementation of a new information system. (Similar but perhaps less momentous work design and policy issues arise when operations are outsourced.)

Because there is so much unanticipated discovery, trial and error—
and the need for creative problem solving—information system
success depends on intimate collaboration between client and outsourcer. Their people and their tasks are highly interdependent.
That is the reason for the stress on creative partnerships; continuing give and take, mutual challenges, and joint exploration.

These partnerships are *not* a technique primarily for gaining
acceptance, or giving people the good feelings that come from participation. They are a requirement for marrying technical and technology knowledge with business knowledge. From inception
through implementation, forthright, even argumentative interaction
is required between outsourcer technical personnel and the client
users who have clear strategic goals and operational knowledge.

Thus, the partnerships in outsourcing information systems are not a
one-shot marriage. The involvement of client managers and IS personnel and lower level users has to be continuous. Otherwise major
omissions and commissions will occur in the design and development
of the new system that will be its doom. The same is true of outsourcing operations. A client only can allow a major gulf to separate itself
from an outsourcer in the special case of very peripheral activities that
do not impact the business directly. For most outsourced operations, a
good deal of continuous monitoring will be required and coordination
interactions need to be frequent. (Good examples are the Airline Package Tour and Alton Publishing cases in Chapter 7.)

Seductive Traps to Avoid

Our research along with the case studies and experiences of the
systems development project managers we studied all emphasized
a small number of temptations to which many unwary managements succumb.

1. Management must be careful when sponsoring very large
   leaps forward that seek to propel the company in one giant
   step into a technologically sophisticated future. Planning for
   continuous, incremental change—modification, improvement, flexibility—has many advantages over "big bangs."

2. Senior executives, particularly, have to be sensitive to the tough strategic issues surrounding the need to balance specialization and integration. Particularly given the complexity and dynamism of computer technology, their companies are going to need the services of specialized outsourcers. But the outsourcer's work can't be neatly compartmentalized from ongoing operations.

3. Given the centrality of information and communication, the "product" of computer systems, substantial managerial effort (time and money) must be devoted to continuously reintegrating the work of the outsider into the everyday work routines and decision making of the line, of business managers. So the numbers, the explicitly defined tasks and objectives in the contract, are there "only for openers."

Big Leaps Versus Continuous Learning and Improvement

Top executives who discover that their companies are badly lagging in new information and communication technologies are tempted to contract for large, "do-the-whole-thing-once-and-for-all" projects. For some, at least, there is the comforting presumption that decision making is a costly management endeavor; the really big commitment is economically as well as psychologically the way to go. As we have said repeatedly in previous chapters, these are the temptations that need to be surmounted.

Here is a summary of the lessons to be learned:

- How truly difficult it is for outsourcers to implement these staggeringly complex programs and the high frequency of failure. (After all, if it was easy, most companies wouldn't find themselves so far behind with such frequency.)

- Even experienced and astute managers have trouble conceiving of how a new system in use will change how they do their jobs. There is a big gap between a visionary plan and reality. To configure the system completely, the users need experience in its functioning; they need to see and touch and feel its dynamics as they go about their actual jobs.

- The rapidity with which this technology moves almost guarantees that the system will be obsolete when it is completed. A few decades ago the Ford Motor Company sought to pull ahead of its competition by building a costly "green field," highly automated eight-cylinder engine factory in Ohio. The facility was an engineering marvel. Regrettably, changes in consumer tastes and rising fuel costs made eight-cylinder engines obsolete shortly after the plant was completed.

- The best systems are those that allow the business managers and users to fully absorb changes and then to keep improving, adding, fine-tuning, and responding to new marketing and production challenges. They may continue to require outsourcers, but the initiative and the shaping of the system change comes from the informed, involved user community. Ideally, as users experience and understand the new technology, they aggressively seek out new refinements to better serve their business needs. *Smart users make for smart systems; dumb users make for dumb systems—no matter how sophisticated the technology.*

- Managers should insist that new systems be designed to foster feedback to users and flexibility. *Feedback and flexibility* need to be the critical ingredients. This then permits the users to take the initiative, in contrast to the technologists.

Success Breeds Success. The ideal is having users themselves feel so knowledgeable and comfortable with their systems that they keep finding ways to resolve their business problems and new challenges by adapting and reconfiguring. Then their own strategic needs and managerial creativity can produce proposals for incremental improvements. This evolutionary process provides for *state-of-the-art functionality.*

With more frequent (continuous) change, the company can ride the momentum of improved technology rather than become over-committed to what soon becomes an inflexible, obsolete technical solution. (Some very major financial services companies have been shocked to discover that their spanking new systems don't accept product changes with ease and may be volume constrained.)

Flies in the Ointment. To accomplish this, a major barrier must be surmounted. Both contractor and client are under pressures to show tangible results (for each quarter of financial reporting). Having line managers "explore" the potential of a new technology may not yield reportable cost savings at the outset. And the conscientious outsourcer investing in educating the client and conducting some trials may have only improved chances of getting a contract, not money in the bank. It takes a good deal of trust among real partners to conduct these fruitful explorations whose real payoff may be at some time in the future. But that longer run point of view is one of the best tests for selecting an outsourcer.

How to Use Technology Specialists
Without Sacrificing Integration

Senior management frequently confronts a tough organizational decision that it handles badly or waffles. And the very guts of the issue has been obfuscated in the current rush to both downsize and outsource. The managerial challenge is getting the right balance between specialists and specialization on the one side and generalists and integration on the other.

Much of our analysis of the managerial issues in outsourcing information systems is really the "how to" of balancing business management goals of tight coordination among functions and adaptability with the need for expertise in new technologies (specialization). Put more simply, sensible companies are asking how they can have their cake and eat it too. How can management outsource those parts of its business it doesn't want to maintain in-house because the rapidly evolving expertise required isn't cost effective? But companies still want and need those services and functions targeted to their unique requirements. In the process, clients also hope to gain some economies of scale (as they pay only their share of a highly efficient centralized activity run by someone else).

Predicting the Future

Based on the research and case studies we have completed, we will make some predictions as to how this tough trade-off will get played out in the years to come. (We are well aware that futurism is a tempting game because most avid readers forget to keep score. And everyone listens intently when the future is being foretold.) In this case, however, the trends are already emerging. And the technology is already in place. We also have the advantage of being able to compare the current surge of outsourcing with a previous abrupt change in the internal organization of U.S. business.

The Parallel Rebalancing of Staff-Line Relations

Fifty years ago, American management sought to "outsource" its people management. This was a period in which some of the first important studies on motivation and human factors influencing employee performance began appearing. Many companies interpreted these impressive studies as proving that the organization's everyday managers couldn't handle this increasingly complex and sensitive task. It required experts, trained in a new technology: human resources.

Now they didn't actually outsource this people management function. Instead, they thought it could be handled completely by *staff* personnel specialists. Line managers would continue to deal with work issues, but anything having to do with people would be shifted over to Personnel. Obviously that didn't and couldn't work. Most technical problems involving work have a human component. Also, personnel staffs can't make decisions concerning selection, pay, and promotions without having a profound effect on line management's ability to meet their cost and output goals.

The best of contemporary Human Resources (HR) practice has a continuing give-and-take as between expert and user/generalist.

There is a reciprocal responsibility for training. The specialist aids the line manager in becoming more sophisticated in the use of good HR techniques. And the line manager helps the specialist to understand what is needed from the company's human resources if the strategies of the business are to be best served.

And Back to Information Systems

Outsourcing computer-based information systems has some similarity to those experiences. Earlier chapters describe failures — when management tolerates the wall separating outsourced information systems development and operations from business managers. In fact, as in the HR analogy, many managers revel in the chance to get out from under any responsibility for information systems. Avoiding having to learn about these new technologies, keeping their hands clean, so to speak, and having the contractor fully responsible, all sounds like heaven to them. Of course, the catch is that almost everything about those systems needs to be of interest to the line manager. As we have said repeatedly, they need to both feel ownership and be continuously involved.

And outsourced information systems are almost as central to business success as a motivated workforce. They need to be "worked" by well-timed and continuing interchanges between the client's user community and their vendor of choice. No information system will be useful if it is not continuously accommodated to the very specific needs of the businesses it serves. Left to their own devices, information specialists can design and operate "good" systems. They are very partial to stable environments — the only problem will be that they will not effectively serve the very specific and dynamic needs of their users.

Growing Centrality of Middle Managers / Technology Users

In many cases, corporate practices have not fully caught up with the computer power now in the hands of middle-level line managers. When outsourcing, many companies still follow the model of centralized IS and IT departments, only now it involves the contractor. Line managers who are consumers of the services being rendered by contractors have powerful and flexible front-end client/server technology (and increasingly the competence) to contribute to the fine-tuning of a new system (or even to do application development themselves). They can also monitor and contribute to frequent changes in outsourced operations in response to the dynamics of their markets and products.

In the years to come, there should be much more frequent contact between these line managers and outsourcing contractors. In effect, the outsourcer will not be further away for communications purposes than the HR department. After all, isn't that what all the talk about virtual organization really means?

By e-mail via Intranet and the Internet, video conferencing, fax, and those dated telephones, users and contractors can stay closely connected. Those contractors who enjoy the ease of being nicely insulated from these demands and questions will gradually lose out to those prepared to be integral to a well-coordinated information system.

A Closing Observation: Tails Should Not Wag Dogs

Computer-based information and communication systems are becoming more central to almost every company. Although some aspects of systems, particularly writing new software, are becoming simpler, the overall complexity and expense of this most dynamic of technologies threaten to overwhelm the business focus of management. The old clichés about tails wagging dogs and carts pulling horses come to mind.

Throughout this study we have sought to provide answers to managers seeking to win the struggle to keep business needs as the focus of information systems development and computer-based operations. For many executives this will be swimming against the tide, but it is effort well worth expending in this most demanding and unforgiving world economy. Too rarely does senior management evaluate a new systems project or outsourced operation in terms of how easy it will be to change, update, and make more *con-*

tinuously responsive to current business demands. Instead, the focus is on how much are we getting today for what price.

Management must recognize that the biggest payoff to the bottom line comes from *economies of knowledge*, not the well-publicized economies of scale. Outsourcers and their plans have to be chosen on the basis of how much they will contribute to the abilities of business managers to manage their businesses.

Notes

Chapter 1

1. Cf. Thomas Allen and Michael Morton (eds.), *Information Technology and the Corporation of the 1990s.* New York: Oxford University Press, 1994.

2. For an excellent overview of the history of this technology, see James R. Beniger, *The Control Revolution: Technological and Economic Origins of the Information Society.* Cambridge, Mass.: Harvard University Press, 1986.

3. The Tower Group report was reprinted in *Forbes*, June 2, 1997, p. 140.

4. One of the few careful studies of the negative user reactions to their outsourced information system vendors is Mary C. Lacity and Rudy Hirscheim, *Information System Outsourcing: Myths, Metaphors and Realities.* New York: John Wiley (paperback edition), 1995 (originally published in the United Kingdom, 1994). See also such recent articles as Elaine Appleton, "Divorce Your Outsourcer?," *Datamation*, Vol. 42, No. 14, August 1996, pp. 60–62; "Outsourced Out of Control," *Info World*, Vol. 18, No. 37, September 9, 1996, p. 78; Thomas Hoffman, "Chase Rethinks Outsourcing Deal," *Computerworld*, Vol. 30, No. 39, September 23, 1996, pp. 1 and 16; Julia King, "Big Britches," *Computerworld*, Vol. 30, No. 9, February 26, 1996, pp. 17–18. (This last article describes a survey documenting the low customer satisfaction with some of the major companies doing systems integration.)

Chapter 2

1. Caterpillar: The Global Competitor, 1996 Annual Report.

2. "Information technology spending per white-collar worker has tripled since 1980 and overall IT spending is projected to increase by 60% over the next five years."—B. Battles and D. Mark, "Companies that Just Don't Get IT," *Wall Street Journal*, December 9, 1996.

3. Seth Schiesel, "Technology Dances to a Business Beat, Merrill Shows," *New York Times*, November 23, 1997.

4. Authors' interpretation of the following: The Standish Group International, "Charting the Seas of Information Technology: Chaos," *A Special Compass Report*, 1994, p. 2. See also "When All Else Fails," *CIO*, International Data Corporation, Vol. 8, No. 12, April 1, 1995, p. 14.

5. W. Wayne Gibbs, "Software's Chronic Crisis," *Scientific American*, September 1994, p. 87.

6. Robert Tomsho, "How Greyhound Lines Re-Engineered Itself Right into a Deep Hole: Computer System from Hell," *Wall Street Journal*, October 20, 1994.

7. UOP is a very well-known, prestigious chemical engineering company that develops new petroleum process technologies. It is jointly owned by Allied Signal and Union Carbide. The story received substantial press coverage because UOP claimed to have found a number of Andersen's project e-mail messages that suggested that they were being plagued by programmer turnover and that their managers doubted the project goals could be achieved.

8. Elizabeth MacDonald, "E-Mail Trail Could Haunt Consultant in Court," *Wall Street Journal*, June 19, 1997.

9. Paul Markillie, "System Down," *The Economist*, Vol. 327, No. 7815, June 12, 1993, pp. 90–91. For more academic research on project failure, see K. Ewusi-Mensah and Z. Przasnyski, "On Information Systems Project Abandonment," *MIS Quarterly*, March 1991; and M. Ginzberg, "Early Diagnosis of MIS Implementation Failure," *Management Science*, April 1981, Vol. 27.

10. *Computerworld*, Vol. 31, No 48, December 1, 1997, p. 2.

11. David Garvin, "Leveraging Processes for Strategic Advantage," *Harvard Business Review*, Vol. 73, No. 5, September–October 1995, p. 82.

12. A survey of clients of systems integration outsourcing projects suggests that, in fact, customer satisfaction is inversely related to the size of the outsourcer. Andersen Consulting, Computer Sciences, and EDS ranked relatively low in customer satisfaction. In fairness, these companies are most likely to obtain the most demanding projects. Julia

King, "Big Britches," *Computerworld*, Vol. 30, No 9, February 26, 1996, pp. 17–18.

13. A recent popular management book documents a case for partnering (and alliances and joint ventures), in contrast to a go-it-alone style, that represents the wave of the future for American business. James Moore, *The Death of Competition*. New York: Harper Business, 1996.

Chapter 3

1. Mattew Wald, "FAA Agrees to Buy New Computer to Control Air Traffic," *New York Times*, September 17, 1996.

2. Just one example is RCA's costly effort to commercialize a home video recorder and player: Margaret Graham, *The Business of Research: RCA and the VideoDisc*. New York: Cambridge University Press, 1986. Older readers will also remember DuPont's failure to successfully commercialize Corfam, the just-like-leather developed in its laboratory.

3. *Wall Street Journal*, January 22, 1996.

Chapter 4

1. Thus, user knowledge and experience are used as the base from which the analysis begins. (What seems like an improvement in flow on paper can often ignore a critical operating need. Only the real user knows the myriad of details and unwritten procedures that actually drive the work.)

2. N. Venkatraman, "Beyond Outsourcing: Managing IT Resources as a Value Center," *Sloan Management Review*, Spring 1997, p. 60.

3. *New York Times*, November 11, 1997.

4. Cf. Financial Executives Research Foundation, *Senior Management Control of Computer-Based Information Systems*. Morristown, N. J., 1983. Also, Henry Lucas, Jr., *Why Information Systems Fail*. New York: Columbia University Press, 1975.

Chapter 5

1. However, some clients have negotiated contracts that give them some voice in who should replace core development team members who leave. Realistically, when projects go badly, clients sometimes use their clout to get the project manager replaced.

2. Cf. *Computerworld*, Vol. 31, No. 42, November 10, 1997.

3. *Computerworld*, Vol 31, No. 32, August 11, 1997.

4. Cf. J. K. Halvey and B. Melby, *Information Technology Outsourcing Transactions: Process, Strategies and Contracts*. New York: John Wiley, 1996.

5. NASA, back in the 1960s, used such incentives with substantial success. See Leonard Sayles and Margaret Chandler, *Managing Large Systems*, 2nd edition. Rutgers, N.J.: Transaction Press, 1993.

6. Thomas Hoffman, "Flex-Sourcing," *Computerworld*, Vol. 30, No. 46, November 25, 1996, p. 70.

7. *New York Times*, July 28, 1996.

Chapter 6

1. B. Caldwell, B. Violino, and M. McGee, "Hidden Partners, Hidden Dangers—Security and Service Quality May Be at Risk When Your Outsourcing Vendors Use Subcontractors," *Information Week*, January 20, 1997.

2. Ibid.

3. Ibid.

4. The data on international projects are based on studies by Cynthia Smith. They have been extracted from her larger study of multinational systems development projects. Dr. Smith has worked actively in a number of international settings as both consultant and project staff. She is currently in the Department of Anthropology of The Ohio State University.

5. For a broader view of these issues, see W. Yeack and C. J. Smith, "Capturing Global Project Investment and Development Potentials" in *Global Project Management Handbook* (D. Cleland and R. Gareis, eds.). New York: McGraw-Hill, 1994, pp. 8–17.

Chapter 7

1. For a typical example of this belated recognition, see Jim Carlton, "Wells Fargo Discovers Getting Together Is Harder to Do: Efforts to Manage Operations with First Interstate Resulted in an Alienated Culture," *Wall Street Journal*, July 21, 1997.

2. Cf. Chapter 4.

3. This was one of the terms the Sabre Group negotiated when it outsourced its widely used travel reservations network. *Computerworld*, Vol. 31, No. 48, December 1, 1997.

4. Thomas Hoffman, "Flex Sourcing," *Computerworld*, November 25, 1996, p. 69.

5. Elaine Appleton, "Divorce Your Outsourcer?," *Datamation*, Vol. 42, No. 14, August 10, 1994, pp. 60–62.

6. Robert Scheier, "Outsourcing's Fine Print," *Computerworld*, Vol. 30, No. 34, August 19, 1996, p. 70.

7. Cf. Leonard Sayles, *The Working Leader*, New York: The Free Press, 1993. A large number of case studies show senior management having no knowledge of the level of uncertainty and ambiguity in their current technology. These require a substantial input by middle managers to "fill the gap."

8. This case is examined more fully in Chapter 9.

Chapter 10

1. For further examples of the dangers companies face using new technologies that have not been perfected, see Leonard Sayles, *The Working Leader*. New York: The Free Press, 1993.

Chapter 12

1. Even as savvy and experienced a company as Fidelity, according to the *Wall Street Journal*, found that its system's ambitions exceeded its capabilities. Cf. James Hirsch, "How Computer-Savvy Fidelity Stumbled in Effort to Develop Consumer Software," *Wall Street Journal*, June 11, 1996.

2. The Software Technology Program, sponsored by the Microelectronics and Computer Technology Corporation as reported in Bill Curtis, Herb Krasner, and Neil Iscoe, "A Field Study of the Software Design Process for Large Systems," *Communications of the ACM*, Vol. 31, No. 11, November 1988, p. 1271.

Chapter 13

1. J. D. Gould and C. Lewis, "Designing for Usability," *Communications of the ACM*, Vol. 28, No. 3, March 1985, p. 303.

2. Cf. W. Yeack and L. Sayles, "Virtual and Real Organizations," *PM Network*, Vol. X, No. 8, August 1996, pp. 29–32.

3. For a good overview of some of the issues we have been discussing, see K. Eisenhardt and B. Tabrizi, "Accelerating Adaptive Processes: Product

Innovation in the Global Computer Industry," *Administrative Science Quarterly*, Vol. 40, No. 1, (March 1995), pp. 84–110.

Chapter 14

1. *Wall Street Journal*, March 3, 1995.

Chapter 15

1. "Program of Pain: This German Software Is Complex, Expensive and Wildly Popular," *Wall Street Journal*, March 14, 1997.
2. Stephen Manes, "When Trust in Data Is Misplaced," *New York Times*, September 17, 1996.

Chapter 16

1. "Painting" simply refers to the ability to arrange data visually displayed on a computer monitor in ways that are most comfortable and productive for an operator. The actual data is being retrieved through an on-line interaction with the mainframe or "host" system or systems.

Index